THEATRE ODYSSEY

Ten-Minute Play Festival, 2006 - 2009

Nigel Publishing

Published by Nigel Publishing, LLC

Bradenton, FL 34209

www.nigelpublishing.com / nigelpublishing@gmail.com

Second Edition, January 2013

Printed in the United States of America.

Cover photo courtesy of Solange Viera
Alexander Horstmann and Chelsey Panisch in PRECONCEPTION by Larry Hamm
Cover photo courtesy of Tom Aposporos
Cale Barkman and Tommy Carpenter in CLAWS & EFFECT by Michael Phelan
Cover photo courtesy of Solange Viera
Trina Rizzo, Sandra Musicante and Donna Gerdes in FORGOTTEN MEMORIES by Eva T. Slane

ISBN-10: 0-9841984-1-5 / ISBN-13: 9780-9841984-1-2

CONTENTS

**Best Play Award
*Honorable Mention

Prologue

Nineteen of the twenty-six plays produced in competition by Theatre Odyssey in the first four years of Sarasota's Ten-Minute Play Festival are included in this book. The other Festival plays have been omitted from this anthology at the request of the playwrights. In some cases, playwrights were unable to locate copies of their work, and, in others, playwrights wished to maintain their first publication rights. In one case, Sylvia Reed's two plays, AMERICAN FLAG and WORKS IN PROGRESS, have already been published by Smith & Kraus, who owns the rights to these works.

This book represents a written record of Theatre Odyssey's success during those first four years. The majority of the plays included in Sarasota's Ten-Minute Play Festival were being produced for the first time, many of them written by playwrights whose works had not previously been seen on stage. By participating in these productions, actors had opportunities to originate roles, putting their own stamp on previously unseen characters.

By promoting both playwrights and actors and by introducing new and innovative works, Theatre Odyssey proudly pursued its mission "to contribute, in innovative ways, to raising the community's social awareness and spirit through the art of theatre, while maintaining a nurturing environment to encourage, challenge, and inspire actors and writers."

Ten-Minute Play Festival

May 22, 2006

The initial Ten-Minute Play Festival, entitled "Embarking," was held for one evening at Art Center Sarasota. Thomas Griffin, Artistic Director, utilized the atrium in the Main Gallery to create a performing space of a runway that divided 104 chairs. The event sold out, and additional seats were added on the night of what proved to be a standing-room-only performance.

Christa Kreimendahl's COULD won for Best Play, an award sponsored by Coast Bank of Florida. Adjudicators were Jack Eddleman, Dr. Nancy Hoover, and Jeffery Kin.

The plays were directed by Thomas Griffin and stage managed by Lori Marsh. Actors included Tom Aposporos, Cael Barkman, Elliot Cohan, John Durkin, Larry Hamm, Joanna Haynes, Neil Kasanofsky, Lori Marsh, Michael Morris, Andrzej Mrotek, Sandra Musicante, Gino Norman, Mark Sieve, and Fred Zimmerman.

Delicto

by

Maureen A. Martin

Directed by Thomas Griffin

with

John Durkin as Brad
Fred Zimmerman as Garry
Lori Marsh as Shannon

CHARACTERS

GARRY, a man aged 30s to 40s

BRAD, a man aged similar to GARRY, GARRY'S best friend. Studly and well proportioned.

SHANNON, a woman of similar age, GARRY'S wife

SETTING

A bedroom.

TIME

8:47 AM, the present.

* * *

Lights up.

GARRY, fully clothed, stands in doorway as BRAD, bare-chested with back to audience, zips up jeans. SHANNON, sitting on the other side of the bed from BRAD, holds sheet in front of her. BRAD and SHANNON have in the moment immediately prior to curtain, been caught in flagrante delicto.

BRAD: This is damn awkward, man.

SHANNON: Garry . . . sweetheart . . . it isn't what it looks like.

GARRY: Shannon . . . have a little class. Don't take me for more of an idiot than I"ve already been.

BRAD: What she means is . . . it's not like we planned it or anything.
It just—happened.

GARRY: And it just happened to happen when I was supposed to be in Tampa all day? When I was safely out of the way and the coast was clear?

BRAD: Not clear enough

SHANNON: What are you doing here?

GARRY: What am I doing here? What am I doing here? I'd say the appropriate question is what are you doing here . . . except that that's fairly obvious. So maybe the question should be how long? How long has this been going on?

SHANNON: (*winces*) Oh, Garry, that's such a cliché. Can't you come up with anything better?

GARRY: Not on such short notice. Will you cover yourself up, Shannon? (*She wraps sheet around her.*) Show a little respect for the dead.

SHANNON: The dead?

GARRY: I see a marriage shot dead in the middle of the room, don't you? It's feet sticking straight up, head lolling to the side, tongue hanging out. Ensanguinated. Life and love sucked out of it.

BRAD: Hey, man, we were just screwing around. Don't take it that seriously.

GARRY: How else can I take it?

SHANNON: What do you mean "just screwing around?" I put my marriage on the line for you. Do you think this wedding ring means nothing at all to me?

GARRY: Apparently it doesn't mean much.

BRAD: It just sort of came over us. We were—like—sitting here talking ...

GARRY: At eight-forty-seven in the A.M.?

BRAD: I'm your best friend, Garry. If you can't trust me ...

GARRY: ... then who can I trust?

SHANNON: Besides, you're supposed to be on your way to Tampa.
What are you doing home?

GARRY: The truck broke down.

BRAD: Aw, man, I told you not to drive it till I had a look at those tie rods.

GARRY: Radiator overheated. Never even made it to the Interstate.
The engine caught on fire and it's a wonder the whole thing didn't blow up on me.

BRAD: Don't sweat it, bro. We'll have it up purring like a tiger again in no time.

GARRY: I don't think so.

BRAD: If I can't get it up—and running—nobody can. I'm the man, man. I can fix anything.

GARRY: Some things don't fix so easy.

BRAD: Oh ... you mean ... hey, you're not going to let this come between us, are you? I mean, Garry, we've been friends forever. Five, ten years at least.

GARRY: All good things must come to an end.

SHANNON: You want to end a perfectly good marriage just because of—of a spark plug malfunction?

GARRY: Yup. I think so.

SHANNON: If the truck needed alignment, you'd do something about it ... not just junk it.

GARRY: I've had that truck a lot longer than I've had you, Baby Girl.

BRAD: You and I've worked on that truck together since high school, bro. We're—like—bonded.

GARRY: Yeah. Maybe. But that's a different kind of thing. Just 'cause you were best man at my wedding doesn't mean you can play Mr. Goodwrench alongside me in the bedroom. I'd trust you with any vehicle I owned. I'd trust you with my life—but not with my wife.

SHANNON: As usual, you're blowing this all out of proportion.

BRAD: It's a little misunderstanding. Nothing we can't work out.

GARRY: Sure. A number of ways to handle this come to mind.

SHANNON: That's better. We're all friends here.

GARRY: Not so much. Not today.

BRAD: So, what are the ways? I mean, besides just pretending it didn't happen and going on like always?

GARRY: You see that as an option?

SHANNON: It could be.

GARRY: No. Not for me. Now, taking up my old 22 strikes me as much more likely. (*picks up rifle*)

BRAD: Except it's kind of illegal to kill or maim your best friend.

SHANNON: And your wife.

GARRY: A crime of passion. No jury from around here would have any trouble with a verdict. They know me ... and they know you, Brad ... and they don't know a thing about you, Shannon ... which isn't a good thing, my dear. Not for you. I'm betting on the home team.

SHANNON: It's messy, though.

BRAD: Especially up close and personal, like this.

GARRY: Ennh. Bloodstains can be pesky, but a little Wisk ... maybe some Clorox ... and the sheets'll be the same bright white as on our wedding night.

SHANNON: You hate messes.

GARRY: It is a bit of a messy situation you've put us in, isn't it?

SHANNON: Me? It's not like I got into this all by myself.

BRAD: Thanks a lot, Shannon.

SHANNON: I'm not going down alone.

BRAD: Besides, Garry's not going to shoot us. (*silence*) Are you? (*silence*) Garry?

GARRY: (*lowers rifle*) Probably not. The day's gotten off to a bad start. Taking you two out would only make it worse.

BRAD: (*reaching slowly for the rifle*) Let me have the rifle, Garry. You wouldn't want to shoot us by accident, would you?

GARRY: Definitely not. When I shoot you, you can bet your sweet ass it'll be on purpose. Now keep your hands off my gun.

SHANNON: Brad, get back before you get hurt.

GARRY: Listen to the little lady, pal, or you'll be going home less of a man than when you came in here. And that might require some serious explaining to Miranda.

BRAD: You'd tell my wife about this?

GARRY: I'm guessing she'll figure it out for herself when I return the damaged goods to her.

SHANNON: You're scaring me, Garry. Brad's right. This doesn't have to be a big deal. We made a mistake. We're sorry. Remember what the good book says.

GARRY: You mean the "thou shalt not commit adultery" part?

SHANNON: Well, I had more in mind "to err is human; to forgive, divine."

BRAD: Is that a proverb—or an old wives' tale?

GARRY: Neither. It's just a quotation.

SHANNON: Well, it ought to be religious. It's like the women at the well.

BRAD: And Mary Magdalen.

GARRY: And the woman stoned in the market place for lying with another man. Yeah ... maybe I'll talk to the church elders about it. Or better yet, keep you under lock and key ... or invest in a chastity belt.

SHANNON: You can't be serious.

BRAD: I practically have a Ph. D. when it comes to picking locks.

SHANNON: Now is not the time to brag, Brad.

GARRY: He who exalts himself shall be humbled. Hell! (*raises rifle*) I think I will just shoot you after all and be done with it.

SHANNON: Wouldn't a divorce be simpler?

BRAD: You'd leave him? For me?

SHANNON: Maybe. Under the circumstances.

BRAD: But I'm a married man. There's Miranda to think about.

SHANNON: You weren't giving her a whole lot of thought at eight-forty—

GARRY: —seven.

SHANNON: Thank you ... at eight-forty-seven, were you?

BRAD: That was then. This is now.

GARRY: So, then, you're planning on turning Mormon and taking on both women. I suppose that could work ... as long as Shannon doesn't mind being Wife #2. And you'd probably have to get a real job if you're going to support two families. I, of course, will be out of the picture.

BRAD: Who said anything about ...

GARRY: No ... shooting's simpler. I'm a clean shot. You know that. It won't hurt. At least not much. Or for long.

SHANNON: I'm thinking you're not really sure how you want to handle this, Garry. And you know, sweetheart, that's okay with me. I'd rather you just weigh the pros and cons of everything for a while longer before you come to any kind of final decision. It's better that way. In the long run. Brad and I, we're just going to leave you alone, 'cause I can see we're kind of confusing the issue by just being here. So, we're going to ... uh ... go now.

She grabs BRAD'S hand and they make a beeline out of the room. We hear the sound of an outside door slamming.

BRAD: (*offstage*) We'll send you a postcard from Vegas.

GARRY: (*sets down rifle and takes out cell phone*) Hello . . . Miranda? They're gone. Come on over. The coast is clear.

(*Blackout*)

END OF PLAY

Sins of the Father

by

M. John Bohane

Directed by Thomas Griffin

with

Elliot Cohan as Father Flanagan
Gino Norman as Vincent Scarola

CHARACTERS

FATHER FLANAGAN, a priest in his sixties
VINCENT SCAROLA, a fugitive in his early forties

SETTING

A large city in the Northeast. A small sparsely furnished room in the priest's house containing a couch, a chair, and a telephone on a small table. The priest has a stole in his pocket. The man has a gun in his pocket.

TIME

The present, late Saturday night.

* * *

Lights up.

FATHER FLANAGAN is sitting on a couch. He frequently looks at his wristwatch and then to the front door. There is loud banging on the door. He jumps up and opens it. A man, VINCENT SCAROLA, falls through the doorway into the priest's arms. He is badly wounded.

FATHER FLANAGAN: Good Lord! What happened to you?

VINCENT SCAROLA: I've been knifed.

FATHER FLANAGAN: Why didn't you go to a hospital?

VINCENT SCAROLA: Too many questions. Anyway, what's safer than a home of a priest? That's why I called. I need you to hear my confession.

(*FATHER FLANAGAN helps the man to the couch, lays him down, and pulls up a chair.*)

FATHER FLANAGAN: What you really need is a doctor, and right away. Let me call one.

VINCENT SCAROLA: It's too goddamn late for that. I know death when I see it. (*coughs*) God, it hurts! What I need now is absolution.

(*FATHER FLANAGAN takes his stole out from his pocket.*)

FATHER FLANAGAN: Yes, of course.

VINCENT SCAROLA: (*mockingly*) Three "Hail Mary's" and three "Our Father's" should do the trick. Right?

FATHER FLANAGAN: It doesn't sound as if you're ready to take confession.

VINCENT SCAROLA: (*grabbing the priest*) What the fuck do you mean, "Not ready." Can't you see I'm dying?

(*Reluctantly, FATHER FLANAGAN puts on his stole.*)

FATHER FLANAGAN: (*making the sign of the cross*) In the name of the Father, and of the Son, and of the Holy Ghost.

VINCENT SCAROLA: Bless me, for I have sinned.

FATHER FLANAGAN: How long since your last confession?

VINCENT SCAROLA: It must be twenty years.

FATHER FLANAGAN: Why so long my son?

VINCENT SCAROLA: I'm not your fuckin' son!

FATHER FLANAGAN: It's just a figure of speech.

VINCENT SCAROLA: Okay. Just don't call me "son."

FATHER FLANAGAN: What do you want to confess?

VINCENT SCAROLA: Killings. A shit load of killings: twenty fuckin' years of it.

FATHER FLANAGAN: But...why?

VINCENT SCAROLA: Money of course. I'm a hit man. For the mob.

FATHER FLANAGAN: You mean Organized Crime?

VINCENT SCAROLA: Yeah. La Cosa Nostra.

FATHER FLANAGAN: My son ... oh ... ah ... I'm sorry. What has led you to do this?

VINCENT SCAROLA: Something that happened a long time ago. When I was just a kid.

FATHER FLANAGAN: What was that?

VINCENT SCAROLA: A priest raped me. One I trusted the most.

FATHER FLANAGAN: Where?

VINCENT SCAROLA: In the ass of course, where do you think?

FATHER FLANAGAN: What I meant was, in what place did it happen?

VINCENT SCAROLA: I know what you fuckin' meant. It wasn't far from here.

FATHER FLANAGAN: Where exactly? I need to know.

VINCENT SCAROLA: I know you do.

(*FATHER FLANAGAN stands up.*)

VINCENT SCAROLA: (*continuing*) It was right in there, on the goddamn kitchen table. Late one night.

(*FATHER FLANAGAN slowly turns around and looks towards the kitchen then back to the man lying on his couch. He bends forward to take a closer look at the face of the man.*)

FATHER FLANAGAN: You're Vinnie Scarola, aren't you?

VINCENT SCAROLA: The one and fuckin' only.

(*FATHER FLANAGAN looks anxiously towards the front door and then to the man on the couch.*)

FATHER FLANAGAN: Why are you really here?

VINCENT SCAROLA: (*pulling a gun from his pocket*) To kill you!

(*FATHER FLANAGAN tries to make a dash for the front door but SCAROLA is able to jump up and pull him back down onto the chair. He points the gun at the priest's face.*)

FATHER FLANAGAN: No! Vinnie. Stop!

(*SCAROLA lowers the gun slightly.*)

VINCENT SCAROLA: You know, I've never understood why life is so fuckin' important to people, how much they want to hold onto it. I've been offered big money not to kill them, but I had a job to do then. And I have a job to do now, only now it's personal.

FATHER FLANAGAN: I'm not pleading for my life. I feel a great relief you're here. Since that night I've been plagued with the terrible memory of what I did to you. I broke a sacred trust and have had to live with it all these years. I wanted to find you but you dropped out of sight. I need to tell you how deeply sorry I am. I want you to understand ...

VINCENT SCAROLA: I understand enough. Shooting is too fuckin' easy for you. They ought to crucify all you holy pedophiles.

(*SCAROLA raises the gun again.*)

FATHER FLANAGAN: Why now, after all this time?

(*SCAROLA lowers the gun slightly.*)

VINCENT SCAROLA: Now I'm dying.

FATHER FLANAGAN: My son, do you believe in God?

VINCENT SCAROLA: If you call me "son" one more fuckin' time I'll shoot your goddamn balls off. Got it?

FATHER FLANAGAN: I need to know if you believe in Him.

VINCENT SCAROLA: What do you think? I gave up believing in your Almighty God twenty years ago. I came to hate everything you and the church stood for. I never got it out of my mind. I'll never forget it!

(*SCAROLA grabs his stomach and coughs hoarsely. He falls down onto the couch.*)

FATHER FLANAGAN: Vinnie, I don't think you're here to kill me. I believe you came here tonight looking for some kind of redemption. I know in my soul that before this night is over you'll get down on your knees and beg Jesus for His forgiveness.

(*SCAROLA winces with pain. FATHER FLANAGAN tries to make him comfortable by tenderly stroking his forehead.*)

VINCENT SCAROLA: Don't you touch me like that!

FATHER FLANAGAN: I'm only trying to make you comfortable.

VINCENT SCAROLA: That's what you said back then. I came looking for help and all I got from you was a life of hell. You were my hero and you destroyed me.

FATHER FLANAGAN: It can't be all my fault. I know your life at home was rough.

VINCENT SCAROLA: Pure fucking hell! My father was a real bastard. He beat me and my Ma every night. It killed her in the end.

FATHER FLANAGAN: Did it get any better once you started school?

VINCENT SCAROLA: You're kidding, right? The shit at home continued at St. Mary's school where the priests beat the crap out of us. You were the only kind one. You worked hard with us kids; teaching us boxing and how to look after ourselves. You used to help me with my homework and got me interested in athletics. And basketball. Boy, did we have some tough games. It started to turn my life around. Then there was that one night. The night you raped me. I was a bad enough kid before but what you did drove me back even deeper into my anger. But I got a job that paid me good money to use that hatred.

FATHER FLANAGAN: Don't you feel any guilt about what you've done?

VINCENT SCAROLA: I've no fuckin' guilt left, just revenge. I can't rid myself of the memory of that night. I just can't get it out of my mind. (*pause*) Before I die I need something, something to rid me of the disgust I feel inside.

FATHER FLANAGAN: I understand how you feel.

VINCENT SCAROLA: There's no way you can understand.

FATHER FLANAGAN: Neither of us chose our parents well. Like you, I had a terrible father. When I was a child he molested me repeatedly. He forced me into a diseased world of deviant cravings. I thought that maybe by taking a vow of chastity I would somehow rid myself of the impulses, or at least contain the evil obsession. You may not believe this, but you were the only one. What I did that one time drove me into an abyss of self loathing. I wanted to kill myself. Almost did. Stuck a revolver into my mouth and started to count to three. Didn't get past two.

VINCENT SCAROLA: What the hell stopped you?

FATHER FLANAGAN: I had an epiphany. I suddenly realized that any fool could die. Dying was easy. It's living that's the challenge. From that point on I dedicated my life to understanding the causes of sexual perversion and to work with other priests who had the same problem. I was able to help many of them.

VINCENT SCAROLA: I don't fucking believe you! You pedophiles, you can't ever stop.

FATHER FLANAGAN: Yes, we can. With the grace of God, we can. Forgive me, Vincent.

VINCENT SCAROLA: Why the hell should I forgive you?

FATHER FLANAGAN: I know what I did to you was terrible. But you have to see that the burden of hate you've carried inside of you these many years has only hurt you. Not me. Forgiveness is the path to inner peace. You have to find it in your heart to forgive me.

VINCENT SCAROLA: Tell me, Father, is it some people's fate to be always unhappy?

FATHER FLANAGAN: (*stroking the man's forehead again*) We're both prisoners of our past. Since that terrible night you and I have lived under the shadow of that appalling crime, and paid for it dearly. I'm as much a murderer as you. Worse even. I killed your soul.

VINCENT SCAROLA: It's funny, but the pain has gone away.

FATHER FLANAGAN: Let me call for help now.

VINCENT SCAROLA: Sure, go ahead.

(*As FATHER FLANAGAN: dials 911, SCAROLA drags himself off of the couch.*)

FATHER FLANAGAN: Hello. This is Father Flanagan at St. Mary's church. Please send an ambulance to the priest's house next door. It's an emergency. Someone's been stabbed ... What ... Yes ... Yes ... I understand. Please hurry!

(*FATHER FLANAGAN replaces the phone. They stand staring at each other. SCAROLA is holding the gun down by the side of his body.*)

VINCENT SCAROLA: Are they coming?

FATHER FLANAGAN: They're on their way.

VINCENT SCAROLA: The police too?

FATHER FLANAGAN: Yes.

VINCENT SCAROLA: That's good.

FATHER FLANAGAN: They'll be here soon.

VINCENT SCAROLA: It's finally over, isn't it?

FATHER FLANAGAN: Vinnie, I'm truly sorry for all the ...

VINCENT SCAROLA: I know you are. I have forgiven you.

(*SCAROLA raises the gun and shoots the priest. FATHER FLANAGAN stumbles into the arms of the man.*)

VINCENT SCAROLA: (*continuing*) I can forgive you, Father, but I can't forget.

FATHER FLANAGAN: (*dropping slowly to the floor*) My son, if you cannot forget, you cannot forgive.

(*For several moments SCAROLA stares down at the dead body of the priest then begins to sob. SCAROLA kneels down and kisses the priest gently on his head.*)

VINCENT SCAROLA: (*lifting his face upwards*) Oh, sweet Jesus, forgive me!

(*SCAROLA falls dead beside the priest.*)

(*Blackout*)

END OF PLAY

The Cello

by

Robert L. Kinast

Directed by Thomas Griffin

with

Neil Kasanofsky as Ralph
Larry Hamm as Larry

CHARACTERS

RALPH, mid-twenties, teacher at a community college, unmarried and unable to sustain a relationship with a woman.

LARRY, mid-forties, music teacher and band director at the same community college, fatherly, a sympathetic listener.

SETTING

The faculty lunch room at the college where RALPH and LARRY teach. No furnishings are needed but if possible, soft cello music plays in the background.

TIME

The present.

* * *

Lights up.

RALPH and LARRY are sitting at a table eating lunch. RALPH stops eating, stares at the audience for several seconds, then turns to LARRY.

RALPH: I hate the cello.

LARRY: Excuse me?

RALPH: I said I hate the cello! That dreadful sound is so melancholy and depressing. (*with exaggerated gestures*) And all that fingering and dramatic bowing. Don't you agree, Larry, as a music teacher, that it's just constipated music?

LARRY: Well, I never really thought about it like that, Ralph. I guess I don't feel very strongly about the cello one way or the other.

RALPH: Well, I do.

LARRY: So I gather. How long have you felt this way?

RALPH: Since the holidays when my girlfriend left me.

LARRY: Which one? Cynthia or Jennifer?

RALPH: Melanie.

LARRY: I don't remember that one.

RALPH: It didn't last very long. She came by my apartment with a bunch of Christmas presents for me. The first one I opened was a CD of a cello concerto by Shostakovitch. To show my appreciation, I played it immediately.

LARRY: Did you like it?

RALPH: I barely remember it. Melanie asked if she could open one of her presents, but I hadn't bought her anything yet. That really ticked her off and she stormed out of the apartment taking the rest of her gifts with her, except for the CD. Now whenever I hear cello music, I feel miserable.

LARRY: Because it reminds you of Melanie.

RALPH: And of Josephine, which also makes me feel depressed.

LARRY: Why?

RALPH: I really thought I had a chance with Josephine.

LARRY: What happened?

RALPH: I met her at a book-signing party last month. I only went because the author is a friend of mine, and Josephine was there for the same reason. I suggested that if we were both friends of the author, maybe we could be friends with each other.

LARRY: Sounds like a smooth opening.

RALPH: It was—until Josephine started going through this compatibility list she uses when she meets men for the first time.

LARRY: Oh-oh.

RALPH: She began with food, my most favorite and least favorite dishes. (*beat*) I began with her eyes which were a soft, pale green, tinged with brown. Very complex and inviting.

LARRY: She didn't ask about musical instruments, did she?

RALPH: We didn't get that far.

(*During the following account, LARRY is gradually drawn into RALPH's suggestive description*)

She asked about entertainment, and I studied her mouth which had well-defined lips that curled down just enough to suggest pouting in a teasing, come-on way. Next she asked about hobbies which made me study her long, slender fingers caressing the bowl and stem of her wine glass. Then there was fashion, which she described by pointing out what she was wearing and, of course, I had to look at her clothes and at her figure which was stylishly covered but certainly not hidden. That's when it happened.

LARRY: (*snaps to attention*) What?

RALPH: I began to hear this low, raspy sound fill the room.

LARRY: Not a cello!

RALPH: "Not a goddamn, lugubrious, doleful cello," is what I think I said. It was nothing BUT a cello! Bach's unaccompanied suites performed by Yo-Yo Ma. And worst of all, Josephine had selected that piece to set the mood for the evening.

LARRY: Ouch.

RALPH: Needless to say, she concluded we were hopelessly incompatible. How was I to know she was addicted to chamber music? To me it all sounds like a swarm of bees caught in taffy.

LARRY: All right, let me get this straight. You're blaming the cello for your break-up with Melanie and your incompatibility with Josephine?

RALPH: There's a consistency.

LARRY: There's a coincidence. You just can't sustain a relationship with a woman.

RALPH: I'm telling you, it's the cello. (*pause*) I was hoping you might help me get a better attitude about it before I see Celeste again.

LARRY: Who's Celeste?

RALPH: My current love interest. Whose father happens to be a prominent cello soloist.

LARRY: That doesn't sound promising.

RALPH: I know, but I really like Celeste. Isn't there something about the cello you can teach me to like?

LARRY: Let's see, you don't like the sound and you don't like the fingering and you don't like the bowing. (*beat*) Why don't you try talking to it?

RALPH: What?

LARRY: Well, if you had a problem with me and thought I was messing up your life the way you think the cello is, you'd sit down and tell me how you feel. Why not do the same thing with a cello?

RALPH: Talk to a musical instrument? People will think I'm crazy.

LARRY: You can borrow one from the music room and talk to it in private so nobody will know.

RALPH: I guess it's worth a try.

(*To the audience as RALPH exits.*)

I didn't see Ralph in the lunch room for three days. Then on Friday he showed up.

(*RALPH enters with a cello and sits down next to LARRY at the lunch table. After a few moments of silence, LARRY speaks.*)

LARRY: Well?

RALPH: Well, what?

LARRY: What about the cello and Celeste?

RALPH: I'm returning your cello, and Celeste is gone.

LARRY: What happened?

RALPH: I took your advice and talked to the cello you loaned me.

LARRY: What did you say?

RALPH: (*talks to the cello*) "Your sound is like sawing wood with an ice skate or listening to a nervous breakdown. Why do you keep interfering with my love life?"

LARRY: And?

RALPH: (*demonstrates as he speaks*) No response. So I touched its strings, plucked them a little, yanked on them actually. You'll have to replace this one.

LARRY: No problem.

RALPH: Then I felt its smooth curves. I leered at its yellow-orange finish. I imagined myself going inside it and looking out at the world enclosed by its wooden sound box. I did everything I could to befriend this instrument. I even took it to bed with me.

LARRY: You what?

RALPH: I put it on my bed while I was sleeping. I thought maybe some kind of subconscious, osmosis thing would happen, but nothing did.

LARRY: I'm sorry to hear that. Well, what about Celeste?

RALPH: You won't believe this. I invited her to my apartment for dinner. When she arrived, I showed her around: the kitchen, the dining room, the living room . . . the bedroom.

LARRY: Yes?

RALPH: As soon as I opened the bedroom door, she let out the most terrifying shriek I've ever heard outside of a horror movie.

LARRY: Why?

RALPH: Your cello was still on top of the bed looking like somebody's fat, snoring uncle.

LARRY: My cello?

RALPH: Anybody's cello. It wouldn't have mattered. Celeste abhors the instrument. She grew up listening to her father practice it eight hours a day. The very sight or sound of a cello makes her want to explode.

LARRY: What did you tell her?

RALPH: I explained that I was only trying to overcome my own aversion to that wretched thing. She said, "You too? I've never known anyone who hated the cello as much as I do." When I told her exactly how much I detest the pitiful belch of that instrument, she hurled herself at me and made the most frenzied, incredible love I've ever experienced in my life.

LARRY: But you said she's gone.

RALPH: She is. She went to her apartment to get her things. She's spending the weekend with me. And I'm going to every music store in the city to buy all the cello recordings I can.

LARRY: But you just said you both hate the cello!

RALPH: We do, but we love what it makes us do to one another!

(*Blackout*)

END OF PLAY

The Grocer

by

Corinne Fleisher

Directed by Thomas Griffin

with

Tom Aposporos as the Grocer

CHARACTERS
The GROCER, a man in his fifties

SETTING
A neighborhood grocery.

TIME
The present.

* * *

Lights up.

I know you're in a hurry.

If you had more time you would have shopped across the street.

But wait. Listen a moment. Only a moment. We've known each other -- from across the counter -- for years.

So grant me the moment.

Yes, I see. Your wife's out in the car waiting for you. Ask her to come in, have a cup of coffee, a pastry. On me. This one last time. She needn't be embarrassed because she's taken her business elsewhere. It's all right. I understand.

Sit down a minute. We'll talk a little, reflect a little. The way we have for years. The way we used to.

Whenever you have come into this grocery store, my store, whenever you have opened the door so that the little bell rings, I've been right here waiting for you. Everything's already arranged for you. All you've had to do is tell me what you want and I reach for it and you pay for it and it's yours.

But before you arrived, before you opened the door and made the little bell ring, and told me what you wanted, something had to take place. Let me tell you about it.

I've had to see that in my store there was just enough of everything and not too much of anything. I have kept the barrels and bins filled with coffee beans and grain and the shelves stacked with cans and boxes. I have petted the cat who catches the mice that may possibly run around at night. And every morning I have a reward for the cat, a special treat.

I have kept the produce bright and fresh. To do that I am at the waterfront market at 4 a.m. When you walk through that front door any time after seven in the morning, you see a dazzling array of the best and the brightest. Gleaming globes of white and yellow onions. Red fat tomatoes. Green bells of peppers. Ruffled heads of greens. I chose them carefully just for you. At 4 a.m.

I take inventory often so I'll know what's been bought, what needs replenishing, what to order, what not to order. And I always have the finest good fresh meat in the display case and the refrigerator. No question about that.

I'm always friendly and smiling -- whether or not my feet hurt or my head aches or I've had a sleepless night or an argument with my wife or a concern about my children or a worry over my bank account.

I go right on smiling. Always smiling.

That horn. The car at the curb. She's waiting for you. A moment longer. Please.

I remember my customers' names. I know my customers. Who has been sick? Who has been out of work? Who is down on his luck and needs to find among the groceries a happy surprise when he gets home --a few more eggs than he paid for, a bag of chocolate for the children?

I remember to ask about your children. I make little jokes with the bread man and the milkman. And inquire about their families as well.

I know what things cost and what to charge. And what the store down the street is charging. And what you will pay.

Though you have come in here almost every day, neither you nor any of my customers has ever invited me to dinner. I'd have presented that night's main course as a gift, along with a bottle of wine. My wife would have brought the appetizer. Chopped liver. Excuse me. Pate. You'd have liked my wife, God rest her soul.

I have never asked myself or anyone what else I might have been.

If ever I had the privilege to yearn, would I have yearned to be a grocer? Ask any small boy -- your little boy -- what he wants to be when he grows up. Will he say, "A grocer"?

This was my father's store. Then it became mine. Nobody asked me what I wanted to be. I am a grocer.

I have always been a grocer. I am used to being in charge, to having responsibility, to managing, organizing. To standing on my feet all day. To smiling all day. Ways I learned from my father. Ways that seem natural and inherited, like the color of my children's eyes.

You've never asked about my hopes and dreams, though over the years, one way or another, you have told me yours. I realize you haven't the time just now to listen. The car is waiting for you at the curb.

Yet you're not leaving. More coffee? Help yourself.

Now I will tell you a dream I have. To turn on the television -- very late after I've closed the store -- to see the President giving awards and medals in honor of grocers and butchers. To see great audiences applaud the prizes given to messengers, street cleaners, trash collectors, housemaids, tailors, bricklayers, dressmakers. To marvel at parades for plumbers, taxi drivers, hairdressers.

My dream. A place where hard work is respected and rewarded and honored.

The horn again. Your car. I understand. You have important shopping to do across the street. A little apple pastry for your coffee?

Across the street, an enormous market. A super market. Two blocks square. There you will find more than produce and meat and fish.

Clothing. Stationery. Hardware. Tires. Bicycles. Toys. Jewelry. A pharmacy. A flower shop. A bank. A market that is more than a market. A city!

I have walked from one end of that market to the other, dazed by the variety, overcome by the daring.

But where are the butchers? Behind glass. To see them, to talk to them, you must push a button and a buzzer sounds. Maybe they will respond. Maybe not. Those butchers scarcely know one customer from another, never remember who prefers what cut of meat, never inquire after the health of the children, the welfare of the families. That store is not mine.

In my grocery store and meat market, my own customers -- old friends, you among them -- have sat comfortably on stools while I waited on them. In a corner, fresh coffee. Fragrant. Real cream. All free. For you.

I move about my store bringing customers' requests down from the shelves while we talk about the news of the day and their lives. Who just had a baby. Who has become a grandmother. Lost a husband. A wife. Had an operation.

Who is thinking about getting married. Divorced. Been to a funeral. A wedding. A graduation. Made a killing in the stock market. Lost a bundle in the stock market. Saw a good movie. Read a great book.

If my customers cannot pay me today, they'll pay tomorrow. Friends. Family.

The store. My kingdom, and I its lord. My breath and heartbeat and blood.

You must have seen the notice in the newspaper, the sign in the window. "Going out of Business."

Now for one last day, I arrange the fruits and vegetables -- fresh and beautiful as a garden. This one last day I set out red meat in beds of green parsley. Another garden.

I offer it up.

Now what can I do for you today?

(*Blackout*)

END OF PLAY

Ten-Minute Play Festival

March 2, 3 & 4, 2007

The second Festival, entitled "Continuing the Journey," was held at The Backlot, a warehouse-turned-theatre designed to provide space for performing and visual artists that did not have access to more traditional venues. Artistic Director Jeffery Kin transformed the space into a 120-seat house and used a play by New York playwright Stephen M. Press, THE GREATEST TEN MINUTE PLAY EVER WRITTEN, to provide a bridge between the other one acts. The final performance on March 4th sold beyond capacity and additional seating needed to be provided.

Jack Eddleman and Mr. Kin directed the plays, which were adjudicated by Murray Chase, Roberta MacDonald, and Dr. Louise Stinespring. Michael Phelan's CLAWS & EFFECT won for the Best Play, sponsored by Coast Bank, but the adjudicators felt that Scott R. Sands' BLOOD AND BONE showed such potential that the play should receive an Honorable Mention at the awards.

Actors played multiple parts during the evening and included, Cael Barkman, Tommy Carpenter, Roz Cramer, Shelby Eddleman, Peter Huxtable, Clair Lockeyear, Ted Mase, Richard B. Pell, Judy Phelan, and Mike Phelan. Ms. Barkman had the distinction of performing in the winning play for the second consecutive year.

2007 Best Play

Claws & Effect

by

Michael Phelan

Directed by Jack Eddleman

with

Tommy Carpenter as Ted
Cael Barkman as Kitty

CHARACTERS

KITTY, a young woman, formerly a cat

TED, a neurotic scientist

SETTING

Ted's lab.

TIME

The present.

* * *

Lights up.

A table is at Center., with a high stool to one side. TED sits at the table facing Left, despondent. The table is littered with papers. TED scribbles furiously, but is weary because he's been up all night.

Enter KITTY after a moment. KITTY wears a cheap short dress with no shoes or stockings. She wears a cloth or velveteen collar tightly about her neck. She slinks toward TED and brushes closely against his back, as would a cat.

TED: (*startled*) Huh?

(*looks about him*)

Oh. I see you're finally up.

KITTY: Kitty sleep good.

TED: That makes one of us.

KITTY: Brush?

TED: Not now, I'm working.

KITTY: Play.

TED: Kitty, I don't feel like playing. I've been up all night, can't you see that?

KITTY: Play chase.

TED: Play chase yourself, will you? Go catch a mouse or something.

(*TED continues to scribble. KITTY circles the table casually, then lays her torso across the table, on top of the papers, facing TED.*)

KITTY: Mine.

TED: Kitty, get off the papers.

KITTY: My paper.

TED: No, these are my papers. See? My writing, my pencil, my papers. Now get off.

KITTY: Play?

TED: Dammit, Kitty! If I do, will you get off the table?

KITTY: Maybe.

TED: Then here. Go get the paper ball. Go, go get it.

(*TED crumples a sheet of paper into a ball and tosses it across the stage. KITTY scrambles after it and pounces. She bats it a few times as TED continues to write. After a moment KITTY looks up, hopefully.*)

KITTY: Play?

TED: (*without looking up*) I just did.

KITTY: Chase me.

TED: Kitty, I'm tired and I'm working and I really don't feel like it. Why do you always pick the worst times in the world to do this?

KITTY: Scratch, please.

TED: I said "no!" Now leave me alone.

(*TED continues to write. KITTY comes around behind the table and rubs her face against his arm, until he stands angrily.*)

TED: God! I cannot do this anymore!

KITTY: Brush?

TED: Kitty – I'm afraid I have some news to tell you.

KITTY: Mews?

TED: Not "mews," NEWS. It's over. Finished. I have to turn you back into a cat.

KITTY: (*hisses*) Ssssss!

TED: Don't you hiss at me.

(*KITTY snarls angrily and comes at TED, claws exposed. TED evades her.*)

KITTY: Mrrrow!

TED: Kitty, calm down. This is not easy for me, either.

KITTY: (*pursuing, snarls again*) Mrrrow!

TED: (*picks up the stool to protect himself*) Kitty, stay! Stay. You stay.

(*KITTY halts.*)

Now, I know it's a shock, but if you'll just calm down and listen, I'm sure you'll see my point of view.

KITTY: Kitty no go back!

TED: Kitty, this whole thing is just not working out. Now, when we first started down this road, I thought I was on to something big. We were going to make scientific history together ... and yes, to a certain extent, we did. But I'm beginning to wonder if it was all just a big mistake.

KITTY: No mistake.

TED: We're not making progress here, Kitty. We've been at this – what – six weeks now? I mean, consider. You shed. Not as much as you used to, but still. You go outside at all hours and you bring back all manner of vermin. Before, it was one thing. I could handle the mice and rats and the occasional chipmunk. But now it's possums. Raccoons. Last week you brought home a deer. What's it going to be this week? A cow?

KITTY: Maybe.

TED: See, this is what I mean. You eat from the floor. Real people sit at the table, Kitty. Real people use silverware, knives and forks and spoons. Real people don't lick their food from a bowl.

KITTY: Me like bowl.

TED: And did you clean your litterbox this morning?

KITTY: No.

TED: I rest my case.

KITTY: Too sleepy.

TED: You sleep eighteen hours a day, Kitty. I don't think ten minutes to clean your litterbox is too much to ask.

KITTY: Not my fault.

TED: (*sighs*) No, it's not your fault. That is exactly my point. It's my fault. Maybe I'm just a bad teacher, or maybe I bit off more than I can chew. But the fact of the matter is, we're not moving forward here. So I need to put it right.

KITTY: No.

TED: Kitty, look at it this way. You can't possibly be happy like this. Think of the way it was before.

KITTY: Me happy. Me tall. Me strong. Me wear pretty clothes.

TED: But only a few weeks ago you could jump nine times your own height. You could see perfectly in the dark. You could turn your ears in any direction and you could hear three times as well as any human. Now you can't even construct a proper sentence.

KITTY: No make fun!

TED: I'm not trying to make fun of you, Kitty. I'm trying to tell you, things were better before. Better for you ... and better for me, as well.

KITTY: Me no bad Kitty.

TED: Grammar, Kitty. "I!" "I am not a bad Kitty!"

(*collapses in his seat, elbows on the table*)

Oh, what's the use? Who was I to play God, anyway? I should have just left you in the alley where you belong ...

(*KITTY rubs sensuously against his back, purring. TED closes his eyes, sensually.*)

You know I can't think straight when you do that ...

KITTY: Bad Kitty?

TED: Kitty, please, I need some time to myself.

KITTY: Good Kitty.

TED: (*stands, agitated*) Go away, will you? For God's sake, leave me alone!

KITTY: Teddy hate Kitty!

TED: No! I do not hate you, and that's the problem! The problem is, despite everything I do to deny it, I believe I am falling in love with you! And I can't handle that.

KITTY: Love?

TED: Yes, love! I've fought against it with every fiber of my being, and the more I struggle, the deeper I fall.

KITTY: Good.

TED: No, it's not good. It is so not good. I am in love with a cat. Physically and emotionally in love with a cat.

KITTY: Not cat. Kitty.

TED: You are a cat. You may look like a woman, but inside you're still a cat, and you'll always be a cat. You see, this is the problem.

KITTY: No problem.

TED: It is a problem. It is precisely the problem, a very large problem. I am infatuated with a woman of my own creation. Not even a woman. It flies in the face of ethics, and judgment, and loyalty, and everything I was ever taught to believe in.

KITTY: You funny.

TED: Look, even if this relationship did NOT smack of bestiality, even if it were NOT for the few ethical standards I have left, you and I could still never work out.

KITTY: Why?

TED: Because you are a cat. And it is genetically impossible for a cat to love anything but itself. And I don't think I can live with that.

KITTY: Try.

TED: I have tried! To my wits' end, I have tried. Listen, do you think I want to do this? Do you think I don't enjoy the feelings you give me? I don't want to do this. I have to do this! It has taken every ounce of courage I can muster to do this.

(*pause, then quietly*)

You know, you're the only person in the world who calls me "Teddy."

KITTY: Teddy play now.

TED: You wait here, Kitty. I have to go get something.

KITTY: Tuna?

TED: An anesthetic. I promise, you won't feel a thing.

KITTY: No!

TED: Kitty ...

(*KITTY blocks TED's exit and struggles to speak correctly.*)

KITTY: I – won't – go – back!

TED: What?

KITTY: I -- .

TED: You used the word "I"! You constructed a proper sentence!

KITTY: I – will – eat – table.

TED: At the table.

KITTY: At – table.

TED: No, Kitty, don't do this. Not now, of all times. Not after I've finally found the nerve ...

KITTY: I – can – love.

TED: You cannot love! It is genetically impossible.

KITTY: Please?

(*a long pause.*)

TED: I need to prepare the formula.

KITTY: No!

(*she grabs TED by the arm*)

TED: Kitty, let go ...

KITTY: Sit!

(*pushes TED down, onto the stool*)

TED: Kitty ...

KITTY: Turn round.

(*turns him to face the table*)

TED: Kitty, if you think I'm going to change my mind ...

(*KITTY begins scratching his back, lovingly. TED moans with pleasure.*)

Oh, God. Ohhhh ... that is so good.

KITTY: You like?

TED: A little lower, please ... oooh, yeah, right there. Ahhh.

KITTY: Kitty stay now.

TED: No.

(*KITTY digs her nails deeply into TED's back.*)

Owww! Cut it out, will you?

KITTY: Kitty stay now?

TED: I said "no,"

(*KITTY digs her nails into his back again.*)

Owww! Okay, okay. Maybe we can work something out.

(*KITTY resumes scratching TED's back, lovingly.*)

KITTY: Good.

TED: (*sighs*) You know what I'm risking, don't you? My ethics, my dignity, my sanity, my reputation ...

KITTY: Me know.

TED: Grammar, Kitty. "I". "I know."

KITTY: Whatever.

(*Blackout*)

END OF PLAY

Duct Tape

by

Corinne Fleisher

Directed by Jack Eddleman

with

Cael Barkman as Pandora
Ted Mase as Mercury
Richard B. Pell as God
Shelby Eddleman as Hope

CHARACTERS

PANDORA, a woman, teens to 20s
MERCURY, a man, 20s to 30s
THE GOD WITH THE DEEP VOICE, an older man
SWEET VOICES IN THE BOX (HOPE and LOVE), two younger women (Rockettes)

SETTING

A city street.

TIME

Whenever.

* * *

Lights up.

Stage Center, a very, very large box wrapped in white paper and fancy ribbons. Enormous gift tag dangles loosely from the side. Atop a tall ladder sits THE GOD WITH THE DEEP VOICE. Facing the box, hands on hips, stands PANDORA. She wears tight blue jeans, spangled sneakers, and a tee shirt on which is printed front and back, "Someday a Woman will be President." She has a very large back pack.

PANDORA circles the box.

THE GOD: Pandora!

PANDORA: Yeah?

THE GOD: See that box?

PANDORA: You kiddin'?

THE GOD: Don't get fresh. This is your Maker speaking.

PANDORA: Okay. I see the box.

THE GOD: Good. It's a birthday present from all of us up here on Mount Olympus. So far there's only one like you down there on Earth -- only one woman.

PANDORA: Cool. Thanks for the present.

THE GOD: You're welcome. There's a caveat.

PANDORA: Say what?

THE GOD: A caveat. A little restriction.

PANDORA: Yeah? Like what?

THE GOD: You're not allowed to open it. Ha! Ha!

PANDORA: (*kicks the box*) Let me get this straight. You and those other guys are giving me a birthday present I'm not allowed to open?

THE GOD: You got it. (*Sparkling confetti, accompanied by a clonk of discordant notes, falls from above.*)

PANDORA: (*rubbing her eyes and brushing herself off*) What was that?

THE GOD: Curiosity. An extra special dose.

PANDORA: Curiosity? It itches. You fellas are real sports.

THE GOD: (*deep and spooky with diabolical laughter*) Remember! Do not open the box!

(*MERCURY in leotard, winged cap and booties, wheels in on roller blades, or a motorcycle, or a tricycle.*)

MERCURY: Hi there!

PANDORA: (*circling the box, kicking it, scratching her neck*) They sent you. You gotta be from up there. What's in the box?

MERCURY: Big secret.

PANDORA: When can I open it?

MERCURY: They didn't say.

PANDORA: I just got born. Today's my birthday. I wanna open my present.

MERCURY: Yep.

PANDORA: And they gave me this super case of Curiosity. It really itches. Phooey! Here I go! I'm going to get at that thing! (*She attacks the box, pulling a ribbon loose.*)

MERCURY: Better not.

(*PANDORA circles the box, tapping, kicking, sniffing. She puts her ear to it.*)

PANDORA: When then?

MERCURY: That's up to them. Don't be greedy. They've already given you lots of presents.

PANDORA: Yeah? Such as?

MERCURY: (*wheeling around, looking her over*) Well, for starts, you're not bad looking. You've already got street smarts, curly hair, plenty of Curiosity, and a cute tush. Not to mention the backpack with all that equipment. They probably figure that's enough for one birthday. You know how they are.

PANDORA: No. I don't know how they are.

MERCURY: They don't make it easy.

(*PANDORA removes a stethoscope from the backpack and holds it against the box.*)

PANDORA: Wow! What a racket! Are you guarding it for them?

MERCURY: Standing by to see that things go the way they're supposed to.

PANDORA: If they're so High and Mighty, how come they need you to guarantee the plot?

(*thunder and lightning*)

MERCURY: Better watch out. They're very irritable and they don't like any back talk. Here's the situation. You're the first woman on Earth. The very first -- this time around, that is. So there may be a few kinks in the machinery. Some unpredictable elements in the apparatus. That's where I come in.

(*PANDORA removes a telescope from the backpack, opens it, and pirate like, holds it against the box. She peers through the scope. Closing the telescope, she puts one eye against the box, then the other eye.*)

PANDORA: This doesn't work. They didn't give me x-ray vision.

Okay! That does it! Stand back! Here I go!

(*She tears a sheet of wrapping paper from the box.*)

MERCURY: I'm telling you, Honey. They don't like to be disobeyed. Especially the head honcho. There's always a price to pay.

PANDORA: Price?

MERCURY: Open the box and you'll release scourges and afflictions you can't imagine. Disease. Misery. Famine. Hatred. War. Greed. Nausea. And forever after your name will be Woman.

PANDORA: Woman. That's bad?

MERCURY: (*all in one breath, if possible*) It means your work will be underpaid and underappreciated, not to mention never done, and what you look like will be more important than what you do, and if you get raped they'll say you provoked it and if you enjoy sex they'll say you're a nympho and if you don't they'll say you're frigid, and if you ask too many questions they'll say you're pushy and if you're quiet they'll say you're dumb, and though men will be planting soy beans, delphiniums, and marijuana on the moon you'll still have to wonder if your contraceptive is really reliable, and when you go to the Ladies' Room at intermission there will be a long line waiting for two stalls, one of which doesn't flush and never has.

(*She screams the primal scream.*)

MERCURY: And I haven't even gotten into Hot Flashes.

PANDORA: That does it! (*kicks the box*) The heck with it! They can keep their rotten box! I'll go find something else to be curious about.

(*She starts for the exit.*)

MERCURY: On the other hand --

(*She stops, turns around.*)

PANDORA: What?

MERCURY: On the other hand, if you can get past all the evil, disgusting, slimy, miserable, revolting, smelly, destructive stuff fermenting in the top of the box, there's something really special at the bottom.

PANDORA: No kidding. Does it need batteries? I think I have some in this back pack.

MERCURY: No batteries. But to get to the bottom of the box, you've got to go through the top! That's the catch!

PANDORA: Think so? They used really crummy paper and tape for this thing.

(*She pushes against the box with both hands. It topples over. PANDORA places her stethoscope on the box's underside.*)

PANDORA: Oh! Oh! Like Wow! I can hear sweet lovely voices singing and sighing, though ever so faintly. Hello! Who's in there?

SWEET LOVELY VOICE: My name is Hope. My sister's name is Love. Please let us out.

PANDORA: You got it, baby! There has to be an Exacto knife in this backpack. Hang in there! I'm gonna open the bottom of this box!

MERCURY: I'm telling you, PANDORA. You'll be sorry --

PANDORA: (*poking around in the back pack*) And they gave me duct tape! Duct tape! The world's mine! I'm gonna tape the top shut first. Tape it around and around, over and over, so it's good and closed forever! And then -- and then -- I'll cut the bottom open with my trusty Exacto knife. I'll release the girls -- Hope and Love -- and I'll keep all that other awful stuff taped up inside this box forever. Just think! No disease, no famine, no wars, no misery! Only the sweet lovely sounds of Hope and Love!

(*She tapes up the top of the box.*)

Wow! I mean like Wow! The world's gonna be a beautiful place! Once it gets around who let Love and Hope out of the box and who kept those horrible other things taped shut in the box forever, I'll be famous! TV interviews, endorsements. You name it. I'll be rich. My names will be Nurturer, Giver of Life, Maker of Hearth and Home, Planter of Seeds, Peacemaker. Ought to be worth a Kennedy Center honor at least. They'll call me ...

MERCURY: Don't get carried away.

PANDORA: ... Chief Gardener, President and CEO, Budget Balancer, Jar Opener, Harbinger of Warmth and Light and Joy, not to mention Mother Earth.

(*long, low rumble of thunder and a flash of lightning*)

THE GOD: Mercury!

MERCURY: You called?

THE GOD: You know the plot. Stick to the script.

MERCURY: But she's determined. And she's got all that duct tape plus an Exacto knife. Can't we do it this way for a change? It'd be such a relief! Just take a look at what happened last time we did it your way. The whole place up in smoke in one big flash. Adios Amigos. Nothing left. Just ashes. And who had to sweep it all up? Who?

(*more thunder and lightning*)

MERCURY: Did you forget? You've been awfully forgetful lately. Not to mention cranky. But then you're old.

THE GOD: Watch your language. I'm not old. I don't get old. It's just that I'm under a lot of stress. All these details. All those decisions. Everybody always asking for something.

MERCURY: What a mess! Creating and destroying, destroying and creating. And forgetting what's already been done. Or undone. And then all the trouble we have starting over -- inventing the Word and the Light and the Morning and the Evening all over again. Not to mention the whales. That's a lot of trouble, inventing whales! You really want to go through all that again?

THE GOD: I'm thinking. I'm thinking.

SWEET LOVELY VOICE: Hello! Pandora It's really hot in here and we've got to pee. Please let us out. We're Love and Hope. Remember?

(*moment of silence*)

THE GOD: Mercury.

MERCURY: You called?

THE GOD: Pandora.

PANDORA: Say what?

THE GOD: I've been thinking things over. I've changed my mind.

PANDORA: So soon?

THE GOD: Wasn't so soon. It's been a couple of eons since Mercury made that totally disrespectful and unacceptable speech about reinventing morning and evening and whales.

PANDORA: Gosh! How time flies!

THE GOD: And if there's one thing I demand, it's respect. Nevertheless, being a merciful God, though irritable and unpredictable, I've been thinking things over. I've decided to try something new and different this time.

PANDORA AND MERCURY: Like what?

THE GOD: Conservation. Fewer automobiles, more bicycles and roller skates and feet. Wind power. Sun power. A chicken in every pot and a brick in every toilet tank. Everything knows how to remake itself or gets recycled. Nobody buys anything new. Ever. Consignment shops do big business. Every store a Health Food store. Put that on a bumper sticker. Nobody gets fat. Nobody goes hungry. Hardly anybody gets sick. Everybody takes care of everybody else and looks after his own garden and keeps an eye on his neighbor's in case of hurricanes. Here. This ought to hold the whole thing together!

(*A new roll of duct tape is dropped from the ladder, along with gold confetti.*)

Maybe I can take a nap now.

Light dims on THE GOD. A few bars of a really loud "Stars and Stripes Forever," as PANDORA rips open one end of the box. Two gorgeous bikinied Rockettes, arms aloft, emerge. From the other end of the box a terrific racket is heard: Scary Things demanding to be set free. The Box falls over with a great thud.

(*Blackout*)

END OF PLAY

Heather's Legacy

by

James Hilderbrandt

Directed by Jeffery Kin

with

Tommy Carpenter as Tony
Peter Huxtable as Jason

CHARACTERS

TONY, a male in his mid 30's to early 40's

JASON, a male the same age

SETTING

A gay bar in Florida.

TIME

The present.

* * *

Lights up.

TONY and JASON walk downstage and face the audience.

TONY: I'm not gay! I'm in a gay bar, but I'm not gay.

JASON: But I sure am. I'm gay enough for the two of us.

TONY: I'm here because Jason asked me to come here. At first it freaked me out, but now I'm used to it.

JASON: I love it when guys think Tony is my lover. Sometimes I let that wrong impression linger, because it boosts my status in here. But Tony is definitely straight. He's a friend, and it's wonderful to have a straight guy for a friend.

TONY: I love football.

JASON: I hate football.

TONY: I tried to teach Jason about football. I took him to some games.

JASON: I tried to teach Tony about art. I took him to a museum.

TONY: I sometimes work on Jason's car.

JASON: I sometimes clean Tony's house.

TONY: We think totally differently. I try to understand his point of view.

JASON: I sometimes tell Tony, "I'll try to see your point of view, but I don't think I can get my head that far up my ass."

TONY: I'm Jason's friend because he saved my life.

JASON: I don't think I saved his life.

TONY: It all started when my wife and my son and I moved next door to Jason.

JASON: The first day, Tony's son, Anthony, walked into my backyard and put his hand into my fountain. I have a huge concrete fountain and it was around Mardi Gras time, so I had beads all over the fountain. Anthony, who was only five years old at the time, put his hand in the water of the fountain, (*mimics limp hand splashing in the water*), and looked at me and asked, "What's this?" I could see how fascinated he was with artistic things.

TONY: When my wife Heather discovered Anthony was in his backyard, she went over and apologized. I was busy moving furniture.

JASON: I loved Heather from the minute I saw her. She was a beautiful woman, and I could see what a devoted mother she was. She loved art, and I told her I was an art teacher, but I was taking time off to work on my doctorate degree. We became good friends.

TONY: Heather told me that Jason had offered to baby-sit Anthony. I told her she was crazy. I didn't want some guy babysitting my son.

JASON: Heather invited me over for dinner.

TONY: (*to audience*) I wasn't nice. I knew Jason was gay, and he rubbed me the wrong way.

JASON: (*to audience*) I knew right away Tony didn't like me. Lots of straight guys don't like me. I never could figure out why. I'm no threat to straight men. I won't steal their women. I can't compete with them in any sport, and sports seem ultra important to them, almost like a religion. I find them physically attractive. They should be flattered, but instead I'm an irritant to them. Why? Are they afraid they're going to turn into me? I doubt that.

Do I remind them of a part of themselves they don't want to exist? I really wish I knew. Or do they think that women are inferior to men, and so if a man acts like a woman, he's lowering himself? I don't know.

TONY: I told my wife, Jason is not going to babysit my son. I don't want that fag anywhere near Anthony.

JASON: Heather cooled things with me. She let Nancy, her other neighbor, baby-sit Anthony. I invited Heather over, and asked why she was brushing me off. She was so sweet. She didn't want to hurt my feelings. She felt a little ashamed, and she and Anthony started coming over. I would have art projects for Anthony to do. I now was convinced her son belonged to my tribe. Heather felt the same way.

TONY: I was working hard and didn't know Heather was becoming a good friend to Jason.

JASON: Then one day Heather came over alone. I had known her for two years. I knew something was wrong right away. I wondered if she had a fight with Tony. I wish it had been that simple. Instead it was more serious. She told me she had been diagnosed with breast cancer. I was the first person she told. She started crying, and then I started crying. But I told her, this is ridiculous. You can beat this thing. I'll help you. You're young. You're in shape. You have a son to raise. You have to live.

TONY: When Heather told me, I couldn't believe it. Her breasts were so beautiful. How could that beautiful part of her body be diseased. I knew she would get better.

JASON: Her cancer was aggressive. She had to have a mastectomy, and then chemotherapy. Her hair fell out.

TONY: Her parents came down from Erie, and stayed with us for a while to help out. When they left, my parents came from Minnesota. When they left Heather was still pretty sick and Jason came over every night with dinner. He made Heather feel better. He joked with her. He made her laugh, something I couldn't do. He was devoted to her. It didn't matter what I thought about him, he was good for Heather, and so he became part of my family.

JASON: Heather got very sick. Physically she looked terrible, but she always looked beautiful to me. She fought with everything she had, but her time was up and she knew it. (beat) She told me things that she couldn't tell her husband or her family, because she didn't want to hurt them with her despair. She made me promise that I would help Tony and Anthony as long as I was able.

TONY: When Heather died I couldn't believe it. I was in shock. I couldn't imagine my life without her. I was living a nightmare. A big part of me had been ripped away.

JASON: We all grieved, and we all do it in our own way. Tony withdrew totally. I knew that wasn't good, but I didn't know how to handle Tony, and I was grieving too. I had just lost my best friend. I babysat Anthony after school once Tony went back to work. I cooked every night for the two of them. Anthony is like a son to me. He wanted his mother. He was confused by her death. He felt abandoned. We became close. He could talk to me. But parenting Anthony increased my pain. One of the worst things that can happen to a child is to lose his mother, and it's a painful experience to watch a child struggling to understand and cope with that loss.

TONY: Jason saved my life. It's the truth.

JASON: Tony began eating less and less. He didn't talk much. I didn't realize how serious this was. One night my intuition told me to check up on him, so after dinner I returned to his house to find him in the bedroom with a gun to his head.

TONY: I didn't want to live anymore. I didn't want to live without my wife. It wasn't fair. She shouldn't have been taken from me. Other men have their wives, why was mine taken away? Why? Heather was a good person. She never hurt anybody. I never in my life experienced so much pain—it was too much. (*pantomimes gun to head*)

JASON: I opened the bedroom door and saw that Tony had a gun to his head. Something snapped inside of me.

(*JASON turns to Tony and recreates the scene.*)

You big fraud. You tough macho wimp. You're nothing but a coward. Faggots are a lot stronger than you are. I know guys that have AIDS. If anyone has a right to commit suicide they do. All the shit they have to deal with physically, and then all the shit they have to deal with from men like you. They deal with it every day. They don't cave in, and they don't have a son to raise. Go ahead, pull the trigger, asshole. Think Heather would be proud of you right now? She fought to the very end. She didn't give in. Go ahead kill yourself. I'll raise your son. I'm the only one in this room with a pair of balls.

TONY: Fuck you. (*Takes gun away from his head and points it directly at Jason's head.*) Fuck you.
JASON: Go ahead and shoot me. You hated me from the beginning. Straight men have wanted me dead my whole life. I'm here trying to help you because I loved Heather, and I promised her that ...

TONY: I ... oh God, it hurts ...

(*TONY puts down the gun, and sinks to his knees and begins to cry. JASON goes over, kneels down and hugs TONY. TONY hugs JASON.*)

I don't hate you. And thank you for helping Heather ... and my son.

JASON: (*to audience*) When a straight man cries in your arms it's an experience you never forget. (*to TONY*) Let me help you.

(*They stop hugging and JASON helps TONY stand up.*)

TONY: (*to audience*) I'll always be grateful to Jason.

JASON: I'll always be grateful Tony didn't blow my head off. Looking back, I didn't act in a very intelligent way, but somehow it worked. Maybe Heather was up in heaven pulling some strings. Sure seems that way. Anyway, I wised up and Tony got some counseling, and Anthony too. It's the one year anniversary of Tony's suicide attempt. It's the one year anniversary of when our friendship began.

TONY: I go to gay bars because I want Jason to find someone like Heather. Well, a male version of Heather. I want the best for Jason.

JASON: I'm trying to get Tony to start dating now. Maybe it's too early for him, but it seems better for him to get out instead of staying home. I go to straight clubs with him--it's kind of ghastly, but he needs a woman in his life. He's very protective of me in straight bars and I try to be protective of him in gay bars.

TONY: Sometimes my buddies look funny at Jason. That makes me mad. I tell them he's my cousin. They don't say anything then.

JASON: I realize that when Tony does find a woman, she may not want me in his life. I will walk away, if I have to, because I will always put Tony and Anthony's best interest above my own. I hope though, the new woman in his life will not feel threatened by me, and realize I'm good for Tony and Anthony.

TONY: I use to wish I could turn Jason straight. I thought it would be easier for him. I wanted him to enjoy the things I enjoy. But I now realize that if I could turn Jason straight, he wouldn't be Jason any more, and I would miss him. I've learned to like him the way he is. Not that he's perfect, or anything. In some ways he's an immature asshole, but in other ways he's an angel. Maybe that describes a lot of us. Now if you'll excuse me, I have to look over this motley group and try to find a guy that's good enough for Jason. (*smiles*) It's a dirty job but someone has to do it.

(*Blackout*)

END OF PLAY

Tide Line of July 15th

by

Connie Schindewolf

Directed by Jack Eddleman

with

Richard B. Pell as Man
Roz Cramer as Woman

CHARACTERS
MAN, tall, sixty-year-old, friendly, jovial until he becomes angry. He doesn't take criticism well and likes to feel in control of the situation.
WOMAN, early sixties, speaks very calmly, does not get agitated easily. A sadness covers her face but when she smiles, which is not very often, it glows.

SETTING
On the beach of Sunset Key.

TIME
July 15th.

* * *

Lights up.

Visible are two heavy beach chairs and a small cooler. A staked turtle nest is a little back and stage left. In the background we see the outline of a huge house with one light on. It is a soft glow at first but as it gets darker, the light brightens a little. The sound of waves can be heard but very low during the dialogue.

The sun has just set. The WOMAN is on her knees filling in a large hole in the sand. The MAN stands behind her about 15 feet.

MAN: (*The sun just set so he juggles the drink in his hand and applauds. The WOMAN continues her work and doesn't look up.*) That was a beauty. (*Pauses, raises his volume.*) Did you see the sunset?

WOMAN: Yes, it was beautiful. (*continues with her work*)

MAN: (*after a pause*) So, are you going to build a sand castle? (*no response*) Are you building a sand castle?

WOMAN: No, I'm filling in a hole.

MAN: I can see that, why?

WOMAN: (*sits back and looks up at him*) Well, large holes on the beach can kill sea turtles. The babies can fall in when going to the water, or the mother turtles may even become trapped as they're trying to come up and lay their eggs.

MAN: No kidding! Well, kids out here were burying each other today and having fun. I don't think they meant to hurt anything.

WOMAN: I'm sure they didn't. (*sits on her cooler after taking out a bottle of water*)

MAN: (*sits on the beach chair*) So, are you with the turtle group?

WOMAN: Not exactly, but I do what I can. My sister was.

MAN: She quit?

WOMAN: No, she died--lung cancer. I took an early retirement from teaching to come down and help her. I learned a lot about the turtles during those two months.

MAN: Seems to be a lot of that lung cancer going around. It got my Dad and my cousin. He was only 45. 'Course I know about the turtles since I live here. My house is right there--yeah bought out the old mom and pop motel that was there in '91 and built my little pad. (*smiles, waiting for her reaction*)

WOMAN: I'm not sure "little" is the right word.

MAN: Only three bathrooms! If I had it to do again, I'd put in five or six. When all the grandkids are here it's a zoo.

WOMAN: I can imagine.

MAN: Would you believe I built this in '91 for $400,000? I bet I could get a million and a half, maybe two million for it now.

WOMAN: Wow. (*unenthusiastically*)

MAN: The taxes and insurance are the killers though, you wouldn't believe!

WOMAN: I probably wouldn't.

MAN: So you live here on the key?

WOMAN: No, I live on the mainland.

MAN: Where 'bouts?

WOMAN: High Tide Mobile Home Park.

MAN: Oh.

WOMAN: But I won't be there for long since it's being bought out to build high rise condos.

MAN: That's a shame. Where will you go?

WOMAN: I'm not sure. A teacher's retirement doesn't afford much luxury, especially since I'm not old enough for Medicare yet.

MAN: How 'bout the cost of that long-term care insurance, isn't that a bite? (*She looks up at him but does not answer.*) So why don't you walk with them in the mornings? They go right by here?

WOMAN: I know, they walk the whole key. My car's been in the shop awhile, and the bus doesn't come down the key. I don't think you residents are "mass transit friendly."

MAN: (*laughs slightly*) I was up real early one morning about 10 years ago, and I saw this little old man walking at a good clip right by here. He stopped to measure some turtle tracks, and I asked him what the sea turtles were good for anyway, and he said, "What are you good for buddy?" and trotted off. The nerve of that guy! Hey, I do my part. I pay my taxes ... boy do I.

WOMAN: I know, you told me.

MAN: I mean, I'm sympathetic with the turtles. I once saw the turtle group lead babies out into the water with flashlights, and now we can't even have a flashlight on the beach.

WOMAN: Well, through research, they've learned a lot over the years. They know light disorients them now ... didn't know that before.

MAN: Like I said, I do my share. I spent over $1,000 two years ago redoing my lighting to be "turtle friendly."

WOMAN: That's good. That's very good. But if you don't mind my saying so, I think you should pull those drapes on that window upstairs since it's getting dark and your light is on. You did say that's your house didn't you?

MAN: (*not taking criticism well*) You oughta be in the group since you're campaigning for them.

WOMAN: I'm just thinking of the turtles--I don't campaign.

MAN: Yeah, yeah, I know (*sarcastically*) only one in a million make it!

WOMAN: 1,000

MAN: What?

WOMAN: Only one in a 1,000 make it to maturity, some say 2,000.

MAN: And just how did they study that? And how do they know that my drapes open are going to kill any tonight?

WOMAN: Why take the chance, if you can just pull them?

MAN: (*getting angry*) 'Cause maybe I want to see out!

WOMAN: But you're down here.

MAN: Look, I think those turtles can take care of themselves. My brother once saw a leatherback female come back to her nest when it was hatching; the babies crawled on the sides of her shell and she carried them out to the water.

WOMAN: (*staying calm*) That didn't happen.

MAN: How do you know?

WOMAN: Well, for one thing, it would be very rare for a leatherback to lay eggs on Sunset Key. It happened once in 2001, but the eggs were infertile. And no mother sea turtle comes back for the babies.

MAN: Yeah, well my brother may be more accurate than your (*sarcastically*) "ONE IN A 1,000!"

WOMAN: Whatever.

MAN: It's really getting dark, guess I'll head up to the house and think about those drapes (*sarcastically*).

WOMAN: I'd appreciate it if you would think about it.

MAN: So, how are you getting home? If the car's in the shop?

WOMAN: I'm not.

MAN: What do you mean?

WOMAN: I'm staying here.

MAN: All night?

WOMAN: Yes.

MAN: But Sunset Key has an ordinance against camping on the beach!

WOMAN: I'm not camping. There's no tent, no blankets, no fire, just me sitting on a cooler of water and snacks--peanut butter on low fat Triscuits. Would you like one?

MAN: Why in front of my house?

WOMAN: It's a good place.

MAN: Why here? (*She doesn't answer.*) TELL ME! (*pause*)

WOMAN: Because it's July 15th.

MAN: So what? Why are you here?

WOMAN: Because my sister used to stay here, when it was the "mom and pop motel." And one year on July 15th she was sitting right here and she saw ... a miracle.

MAN: What? (*pause*) What did she see? (*She still doesn't answer.*) Look, you're on my property and I want to know what you're doing here!

WOMAN: I'm not on your property.

MAN: That is my house and these are my beach chairs, and I own this, lady!

WOMAN: (*calmly*) No, this is below the high tide line.

MAN: What?

WOMAN: See that thin rack of sea weed up there? That was the last high tide and everything Gulfside of that does not belong to you, including the property your chairs are on right now.

MAN: Are you telling me just because we're having high tides right now that I'm losing property?

WOMAN: I guess you could say that.

MAN: So during high tides I have less land and my property is worth less?

WOMAN: The value of this beach cannot be calculated and you don't own it.

MAN: Who does? The turtle group I suppose?

WOMAN: No, no one owns it...and everyone owns it.

MAN: You're crazy.

WOMAN: Maybe.

MAN: (*Pauses, starts to turn away toward his house, then stops and turns.*) What miracle? (*She doesn't respond.*) What miracle did your sister see here July 15th? (*pause*) Look, I'm sorry. You environmentalists or tree huggers or whatever you want to be called--you do good work. I know it's volunteer and we should all be more concerned about the ozone and the trees and the animals. (*pause*) So, what did she see?

WOMAN: I told you, a miracle.

MAN: Well, if she saw it here in front of my house don't you think I deserve to know?

(*He pauses and gives up finally and starts toward his house. She waits until he has turned, and she walks toward one of his heavy chairs and begins dragging it back. He must hear her because he turns around and starts back.*)

You may be able to sit there all night but those are my chairs, and I didn't say you could use them.

WOMAN: I'm not using them; I'm just moving them back by the vegetation, out of the way of any turtles. Those babies up there in that nest deserve a straight path to the water, and a mother turtle could get tangled. My sister saw it once.

MAN: I'm beginning to dislike your sister immensely. These are my chairs!

(*He stops her by taking a hold of the other side of the chair and pulling. She doesn't let go. They struggle for a minute in a tug of war, eyes fixed on one another until he lets go on purpose and actually pushes in anger. She falls back, chair on top of her. She lets out a moan of sorts. He hesitates, then comes to his senses, pulls the chair off her, and reaches down to help her up. She hesitates before putting out her hand for him to help her. Once up, she brushes sand off, sits back on the cooler, and puts her head in her hands.*)

MAN: Are you all right? I didn't mean for you to fall, I just got carried away. I'm sorry.

WOMAN: I know.

MAN: Look, I'll pull the chairs back. Maybe not every night, until they make me, but tonight no turtles will die on my property because of me. See, I'm pulling them back. (*He proceeds to pull the chairs back and then walks slowly back behind her.*) Goodnight.

WOMAN: Goodnight. (*He starts to walk away. She puts her head up.*) The miracle?

MAN: What? (*He turns back to her.*)

WOMAN: Do you want to know what happened on July 15th?

MAN: Yes.

WOMAN: It was about 1:00 A.M. She couldn't sleep and had come out for a smoke, never could quit, poor thing. (*pause*)

MAN: And?

WOMAN: She was staring out at the waves when she saw a large, dark figure emerge. It lumbered slowly up the beach. She froze. The turtle wasn't startled by her since she was so still. Slowly she crawled within

4 feet of my sister and started rocking back and forth, anchoring herself down for her labors. Soon she was digging, carefully lifting sand out with her hind flippers, and she made the perfect hole for her eggs. As the eggs were silently dropping, my sister's head turned unknowingly to the other side, and out of the sand boiled up in spurts, a total of a hundred or more baby turtles very quickly, and they speedily headed to the water. It was an unmarked nest that was hatching at the same time and within 15 feet of the mother turtle laying eggs. My sister could hardly stay still as she wavered between watching eggs being laid and babies scurrying to the water for their first taste of their home, the Gulf.

MAN: That must have been something.

WOMAN: She said it was the greatest experience of her life. For the hour it took that 300 lb. mother turtle and for the five minutes it took that nest to pop 100 babies, she felt ageless, timeless, as if she had seen God touch the sand and go, and she was part of it. (*pause*) She told me this the week she died. She wanted me to experience it too. She said it was better than drugs--and she would know. July 15th, she said, was about the beginning of nest hatching, and yet the mammas were still coming in strong until later in the month. So, tonight might be the night, and that marked nest back there is due anytime.

MAN: I understand. (*pause*)

WOMAN: One more thing. (*He turns, very interested.*) She said while the big turtle was laying eggs, it had tears streaming down its face. (*pause*)

MAN: Thanks for telling me. Goodnight.

WOMAN: You're welcome.

(*MAN walks back and disappears. The light that shown through his window goes out because he turned it off. The WOMAN sees this and slowly turns her gaze back out to the water, waiting. Her eyes are misty*).

(*Blackout*)

END OF PLAY

Ten-Minute Play Festival

March 16, 2008

The third Festival, entitled, "Chasing the Horizon," was held at Players Theatre, the only occasion up to that time that Theatre Odyssey had utilized a proscenium stage for any of its events. The 2008 Festival included two performances, one in the afternoon and one in the evening. The adjudicators, Rick Kerby, Scott Keys, and Annie Morrison, attended the afternoon event and spoke briefly afterwards. The announcement of the awards was made after the evening performance.

PRECONCEPTION by Larry Hamm won for Best Play and Eva T. Slane's FORGOTTEN MEMORIES received Honorable Mention. Both awards were sponsored by Home Resource.

Preston Boyd was the Artistic Director and was joined in directing the plays by Jack Eddleman, Dr. Louise Stinespring, Pam Wiley, and Fred Zimmerman. Actors included David (Kyle) Abolafia, Tom Aposporos, Cael Barkman, Angel Borthos, Laine Forman, Donna Gerdes, Alexander Horstmann, Ted Mase, Jasmine (Jaszy) McAllister, Kaylene McCaw, Karle H. Murdock, Sandra Musicante, William Muzzillo, Chelsey Panisch, Richard Pell, Trina Rizzo, Cliff Roles, Nadia Watts, and Laurie Zimmerman.

2008 Best Play

Preconception

by

Larry Hamm

Directed by Preston Boyd

with

Alexander Horstmann as Sperm
Chelsey Panisch as Egg

CHARACTERS

EGG: a woman of child-bearing years

SPERM: a man of like age

SETTING

The place is the locus of all human beginnings, depicted by an elevation on center stage.

TIME

Pre-conception.

* * *

Lights up

EGG stands elevated slightly on Center stage, biding her time. SPERM, noticeably shorter with the elevation, swims toward her wiggling his tail. As SPERM nears EGG, she holds up her hand and he bounces off.

Periodically and persistently, throughout the play, SPERM should make an attempt to reach EGG, only to be repelled until the final moments of the scene.

SPERM: Can I buy you a drink?

EGG: Do you have any idea how many times I've heard that line? Over two million in the last 45 seconds alone.

SPERM: I just want to get to know you better.

EGG: Yeah, right.

SPERM: But you have such beautiful eyes.

EGG: Listen. Stop. We both know why we're here, and it isn't to make small talk. I've got a major decision to make, and not a heck of a lot of time to make it in. At best, I've got 24 hours, and given my producer's sex life, my guess is that I'm going to have to choose from whatever's coming my way at the moment.

SPERM: You've got a producer, too?

EGG: Sure. Did you think you were swimming up a sewer drain?

SPERM: (*looking around somewhat stupidly*) I guess I didn't care.

EGG: Naturally, you didn't. Your kind has only one thing on its mind, and we know what that is.

SPERM: We do?

EGG: Fertilization. Being the best of the bunch. Breaking through my soft but resistant outer layer before any of the others.

SPERM: (*he attempts, she resists*) That sounds fun.

EGG: (*pantomimes watching someone approach and go past*) Whoa!

SPERM: What?

EGG: Did you see the tail on that one?

SPERM: No.

EGG: Why are all the really hot ones too stupid to find their way here?

SPERM: That's not the way this works, you know.

EGG: What do you mean?

SPERM: I mean that the one that figures out the way to get to your heart has to be strong and has to defy incredible odds just to find you. Then, while the others strain futilely to win your affections, the best and most suitable (*he points with both fingers toward himself*) works his way in.

EGG: So you think you're the one for me, huh?

SPERM: I'd just like to give you a hug.

EGG: Don't even start. There are a ton of things to discuss first.

SPERM: Like what?

EGG: Like whether I want to go through with this at all.

SPERM: Really?

EGG: Yes, really.

SPERM: You have doubts.

EGG: I have doubts.

SPERM: I have no doubts.

EGG: Of course you don't. Having doubts would mean you've thought about this, and you clearly haven't. You're so caught up in the race to the finish line that you haven't taken the time to determine if the prize there is worth winning. Really, do you have any idea what will happen if I let you in?

SPERM: Nope.

EGG: Well, for a moment we're fused together ...

SPERM: (*excitedly*) Oh yeah.

EGG: ... into a zygote.

SPERM: A what?

EGG: A zygote, a cell that contains all the chromosomal information from both of us. At that moment, the two of us are responsible for selecting one of the over 17 trillion possible genetic combinations provided by our producers.

SPERM: That's our choice?

EGG: Well, I don't know that I'd call it a choice, but ultimately we're the source. The buck starts here. Or the doe ... but you get my point.

SPERM: I do?

EGG: C'mon. Stop wriggling for a moment and think about your role in all of this. Do you want to bring the world the next mass murderer? The next corporate criminal? The next person in the grocery line who waits until after the cashier gives the total to search for her checkbook?

SPERM: My God no!

EGG: I thought not. And who's to say that once you and I were to begin that series of mitotic cell divisions that ultimately creates a human being, that our human being, the result of our union, would be anything more than another body chewing up the planet's resources while excreting litter on a highway or gum into a urinal?

SPERM: You make it sound horrible. And hopeless. After all, what can I do about any of this?

EGG: What can you do? You're begging to be half the equation here, buddy. You'd better start taking your responsibilities seriously.

SPERM: I will. I do. Oh, can't we talk about this after?

EGG: Tell me, what's the scoop on your producer?

SPERM: My producer? Why bring him into this?

EGG: Well, the shape you're in is greatly influenced by his diet and the amount of exercise he gets.

SPERM: (*pulling in his stomach and examining himself*) I think he's okay.

EGG: Is he a smoker? An alcoholic? A drug addict? Is he a Meth Fiend?

SPERM: No! (*realizing he's responded reflexively*) I don't think so.

EGG: You don't think so. C'mon, just what do you know about this guy?

SPERM: Not much, really. I've only been with him a short time. And there are so many of us that he doesn't provide us with any individual attention. He'd ignore us entirely if he didn't seem so preoccupied with getting rid of us.

EGG: So he's heartless and uncaring?

SPERM: I can't say that. For my part, I never tried to bond with him either. I've spent most of my time sizing up my competition and trying to get into good position whenever the opportunity arose.

EGG: And is he the kind of guy who's had lots of opportunities to rise?

SPERM: He seems to. There's a constant call for reinforcements.

EGG: So, he's a philanderer. What a perfect model for half of a genetic code.

SPERM: Wait! I don't think it's like that. It's more like ...

EGG: ... like? Like what?

SPERM: I ... uh ... only have heard things.

EGG: Such as ...?

SPERM: Well, among the guys, there's a rumor that most of us get sacrificed to practice runs.

EGG: Practice runs? Why would he need practice?

SPERM: I don't know, and I can only imagine the disappointment on my friend's faces ...

EGG: Ewww!

SPERM: What?

EGG: So he's a loser.

SPERM: Well, that doesn't seem fair.

EGG: Fair? Don't you see the burden that I have to bear? Do you think that I want my producer impregnated by some geek who might be better suited to a virtual relationship online?

SPERM: No, what I'm trying to say is that you seem to take everything the wrong way. You want to assume he's either a bad boy or someone so benign that he's not worthy of your acceptance.

EGG: I guess you could be right.

SPERM: According to what I hear you saying, he has only two options, and both of them result in your negative opinion. Whether he's sending us on a meaningful mission or out into space, you seem to feel he's misusing his assets. You want him to have experience, just not too much.

EGG: I suppose I am being a bit selfish.

SPERM: And what do we know about your producer?

EGG: Hmmm ... Well, she's single again, after one disastrous marriage and a series of questionable boyfriends. She likes spicy foods (*she reacts to the foods*) and prefers the pill as a form of birth control in combination with a condom.

SPERM: (shudders) I hate those.

EGG: And, apparently judging from her recent decision to go off the pill and your current presence, she's decided that she's reached a time in her life when she should conceive a child.

SPERM: She wants to get knocked up?

EGG: She wants to experience the miracle of birth and the wonders of raising a child.

SPERM: Sounds like she wants to trap my guy with the miracle of DNA testing and the wonders of a paternity suit.

EGG: That's mean!

SPERM: Well?

EGG: I don't know. Things have been so crazy lately. You spend almost forty years with someone and you think you know her. Then, suddenly she's taking a singles cruise and having her breasts enlarged.

SPERM: Those aren't real?

EGG: (*gradually becoming emotional*) And now I'm staring at this. (*motions toward SPERM*) How can I make a rational decision?

SPERM: I realize this is an emotional time for you. If nature were just, we'd have weeks to talk about this.

EGG: (*getting ready to let go*) I'm under a lot of pressure.

SPERM: Of course, you are. But, you're not alone.

EGG: (*letting go and crying*) I just don't know anything about this guy!

SPERM: Hey, hey now, I'm here, aren't I? That's got to say something about his personality and perseverance. He must be someone she's attracted to.

EGG: (*still crying*) Maybe she just got drunk.

SPERM: Or, maybe she likes him.

EGG: (*composing herself*) You're right. You're right. I'm being paranoid. It's just that I'm a bit touchy about such things. She doesn't have the best track record when it comes to men. And the first thing I do when I see a whole bunch of you fellas swimming my way is to question what was on her mind for the past hour.

SPERM: Don't you think it's possible that she's found someone she loves? That the past hour was spent with soft music, a bottle of wine, and a jar of lubricating cream?

EGG: Love? Do you actually think it's that simple? My girl is thirty-eight for chrissakes. She's been through the fumbling years, the experimental years, and the seduction years. She's now in the my-God-I'm-going-to-die-alone years.

SPERM: It can't be all that bad.

EGG: What would you know? Sure, you've the mind, the anatomy, and the shelf life of an amoeba, but your producer doesn't. He doesn't have to worry about becoming meaningless and invisible long before he dies. He'll never feel the desperation that can come with being female. A man such as yours can always find some young uterus to attend to, even until his eighties.

SPERM: Hah! As long as he has a flush bank account and a sports car.

EGG: And that means?

SPERM: It means that for every man that mates there's a woman on the other side. Women help to set the standards men live down to. Ninety percent of what men do is done to get female attention. Do you think that men want to go about posturing and preening, acting tough, and buying oversized pick-up trucks just so they can impress a woman enough to get laid?

EGG: Well, maybe.

SPERM: And do you think that men like the fact that once they've wooed the woman, they have to take on the burden of acting like adults, when anyone can tell you that no man was meant to become one.

EGG: I hadn't thought about ...

SPERM: Do I have to mention shorter life spans? Must I tell you about coalmines, steel mills, and machine shops? Military service? And how about those who work eighty-hour weeks to climb the corporate ladder, sucking in the fumes from their boss's backside, while they do all they can to make sure the missus is dressin' fine and livin' well.

EGG: Women work too!

SPERM: (*immediately*) But do they kill spiders?

EGG: Ooo ...

SPERM: I know women work, and some of them are heroic, but that's not my point. My point is that women can be sexy just being themselves, but men have to be somebody else. If a woman wants to attract men, she buys a pair of low-cut jeans or a short skirt. If a man wants to attract women, he has to work it into conversation that being an Accountant at XYZ Company earns him $80,000 a year. (*pause*) Or, he just lies and says he plays for the Dallas Cowboys.

EGG: You're very passionate about this.

SPERM: I'm not trying to choose sides here, but I think it's important to establish that it's not just women who suffer. There are a lot of hopelessly solitary men out there, but they're poor or they're shy or they're just plain worn out by a series of relationships that always end with an argument over somebody's mother or a fight over toiletries.

EGG: But guys can have those relationships and those fights for most of their lives. Biologically, women have a limited window of opportunity.

SPERM: Men can't help it if they're winning the war against Erectile Dysfunction.

EGG: It's more than that. Women are defined by their bodies. You said it yourself: they're measured by how they look in "low-cut jeans" and "short skirts." What if a woman likes reading books and happens to hate starving herself to fit into a size 2? Is it right for her to be overlooked for a chemically created blonde with a tattoo above her ass that says, "use me."

SPERM: No, it's not.

EGG: You're somewhat sensitive, aren't you?

SPERM: Is that a good thing?

EGG: Yeah, it is.

SPERM: I guess we can agree that men and women both have it tough.

EGG: They do. I don't know if I'd want to become a boy or a girl. (*smiles*) But, at least I'm not responsible for that.

SPERM: I know, I know, and I don't have a clue if I'm carrying an X or Y chromosome. (*he turns around trying to see his back*) I wish I knew.

EGG: You do? I don't. I think I'd like the surprise.

SPERM: Then, you're considering me.

EGG: I never said I wasn't.

SPERM: Our child will be special, you know. Maybe he or she will be able to change some of this.

EGG: Do you really believe that?

SPERM: I think you have to.

EGG: So you think we should?

SPERM: I do.

EGG: (*holding out her arms*) I do, too.

SPERM: (*stepping into her arms slowly*) I'll be gentle.

EGG: (*grabbing his head and pulling him toward her*) Don't you dare.

(*She wraps her leg around him.*)

(*Blackout*)

END OF PLAY

2008 Honorable Mention

Forgotten Memories

by

Eva T. Slane

Directed by Jack Eddleman

with

Sandra Musicante as Annemone
William Muzzillo as Leo
Kaylene McCaw as Erika
Trina Rizzo as Moni
Donna Gerdes as Detti
and with Erika Hendrickson Boyd as the Cellist

CHARACTERS

ANNEMONE, woman, sixties or older. MONI grown up
LEO, man, mid-forties, an opera singer
ERIKA, woman, mid-forties
MONI, 10-year-old girl with dark short hair, reminiscent of Anne Frank in looks. The younger ANNEMONE
DETTI, A Nanny
CELLIST

SETTING

America and Vienna. The characters can all use a slight accent. Though appropriate this is not absolutely necessary. I have inserted a number of words which do need to be pronounced in German (e.g. Amerika, Monichen, Mutti, Pappa, Kind, Kindchen).

TIME

1938.

MUSIC

WIEN, WIEN, NUR DU ALLEIN (VIENNA, CITY OF MY DREAMS) by Rudolf Sieczynski -- played, if possible, by a Cello

* * *

Music up. Introductory section to "WIEN, WIEN NUR DU ALLEIN" plays slowly and dreamily.

PRELUDE

Lights up.

ANNEMONE stands upstage of MONI.

ANNEMONE: There is so much I have forgotten. But the feelings -- they don't go away. They remain. (*moves to stand behind MONI*) I was too young to understand it all then. And now it all seems like a long forgotten dream.

SCENE 1

(*LEO in America, at desk -- writing, ERIKA in Vienna, reading.*)

LEO: (*Stops, looks up to think, then continues writing.*) My Dearest, As I write to you from Amerika I miss you terribly and I miss our MONICHEN. And how is Detti? Is Moni still clinging to her Nanny so completely? Being away from you three becomes more difficult with each newspaper report I read of what is happening in Vienna, in my beloved Wien. I look for news of what is happening in Wien. I look for news every day, but not too much is written in the newspapers, and my English is not good. I worry how serious the situation will become now that the Nazis are in Austria. Our tour goes well, reviews are good and audiences are loving the operas and us ...

ERIKA: (*Reads from the same letter.*) ... but I cannot wait to come home and embrace you and to lift Moni up in my arms again. Do you remember how when she was little I used to throw her high in the air, and how she squealed flying down safely into my waiting arms? (*laughs*) Soon now the tour will end and I will be coming home.

SCENE 2

MONI: Detti, why is Mutti so worried when she gets a letter from Papa? When is he coming home?

DETTI: Soon now. Soon we will all be together again.

MONI: He has been gone so long -- I can hardly remember him.

DETTI: Six months IS a long time for you. But when you see him again it will seem like yesterday. And just think, he is being admired by so many people. You remember how beautifully he sings. (*If possible, fade in a baritone voice singing scales.*)

MONI: Yes. I loved hearing him practicing at home. Even when he just sang the notes, he called it ... (*trying to think of the word*) he called it vocalizing, it was thrilling.

DETTI: Well soon you will be hearing him sing again.

SCENE 3

LEO: (*writing*) Dear Ones, with all the turmoil in Wien the plans have changed. We are not coming back to Wien, but will try to stay in Amerika.

ERIKA: (*speaking to DETTI*) News from Amerika is both good and bad. Leo is not coming back home as planned. The company's contract has been renewed and they will be going on another opera tour. They have had great success and audiences are clamoring for more.

DETTI: That IS wonderful news. It is becoming so dangerous here in Wien. But Moni will be so disappointed not to see her Papa as we promised. How will you break the news to her?

ERIKA: No Detti. Please, you tell her. I would not know how to explain it to her. I could not hide my disappointment. You are closer to Moni. You understand her. You will know how best to tell her. She loves you so much. (*with a smile*) You know, sometimes I am a little jealous of you.

SCENE 4

LEO: (*writing*) Every one here is talking about Kristallnacht -- the night of broken glass! How ominous that sounds. Are you safe? I hear that many Jewish businesses have been destroyed. Tell me about my parents.

ERIKA: (*writing*) We are safe, and so are your parents. But their store has been vandalized and won't be allowed to reopen. Moni was devastated that she will not see her Papa when we told her that you are not coming home after all.

SCENE 5

(*DETTI and MONI rush into the house from outside. They are out of breath and frightened.*)

ERIKA: (*who has been nervously pacing*) Thank goodness you are back. I was so worried about you. What has happened?

MONI: Oh Mutti -- it was dreadful. There we were, just Detti and I, walking and telling jokes and laughing. You know, just having a good time. I love to laugh with Detti. Well, all of a sudden there were these men in uniform standing in our way.

DETTI: Oh they were just boys up to no good. That Hitler Youth Gang, Lausbuben who had nothing better to do than frighten a young child.

MONI: They were saying terrible things. Asking if we were Jewish and calling us bad, terrible names. They frightened me.

DETTI: Well, they did not frighten me. I told them off. I said that I was a good Catholic and they were nothing but hoodlums. Frightening an innocent little girl and trying to frighten me. Well they did not succeed and I told them so.

ERIKA: That was a dangerous thing to do Detti. You must be careful. There is no telling what they would do to you.

MONI: Then Detti took me by the hand and we hurried back here -- they followed us all the way, yelling and screaming at us. But Detti stood her ground -- she was magnificent. What would I do without my Detti?

ERIKA: Yes Kindchen. What would we all do without our Detti?

SCENE 6

LEO: (*writing*) It was a relief to hear that you are safe -- for now at least. We must face what is ahead of us. I cannot come back to Wien, I am sure you know that. Our beloved Wien -- it does not exist anymore. You must leave and join me just as soon as possible. The most important thing is for you to be safe and for us to be together again.

ERIKA: (*writing*) The mail is getting more and more erratic. Each letter I fear will be the last delivered. You say nothing about Detti. We cannot leave her behind. What will Moni do without her?

LEO: (*writing*) Getting the needed papers for both of you was difficult. Getting them for Detti is impossible. And we can't expect her to leave her fatherland, to leave all she knows and loves.

SCENE 7

ERIKA: Detti, I don't know how to tell you this. We will be going to Amerika to join Leo. He has been able to get Visas and sponsorship for me and for Moni.

DETTI: (*after a pause*) I have been expecting this. I have known for some time that the day will come when you must leave, and leave without me.

ERIKA: Yes. There is no way we can take you with us. It will be hard on Moni to leave her grandparents, her friends, all of her toys, but most of all to leave you, her beloved Detti.

DETTI: Knowing Moni will be safe is all I want. I want my Kind to grow up where it is safe, where she will never need to be afraid again, where she can forget all that has frightened her here. Maybe she will remember me. I know I will never forget her, or you Frau Erika und Herr Leo.

SCENE 8

(*ANNEMONE stands behind MONI who is on a train*)

ANNEMONE: Memory -- There is so much I have forgotten. But this I remember. I am confused, abandoned, lost -- on a train heading into the unknown. I clutch my doll with her golden hair and blue eyes. Her beautiful ceramic face is how I want to look, and how I know I do not look. I with my frightened pale face, so different from the glowing pink face of my doll. There is so much I do not know. Just that I have to leave -- leave everything I know and love. The hardest thing is leaving my beloved Detti -- who has always taken care of me. How will I be able to sleep without her tucking me in, without her being with me? And who is this stranger? Oh yes, it is the actress, my Mother -- (*sarcastic*) my glamorous, distant mother. What does she know about me? It should be Detti with me, not this (*spitting out the word*) "lady." What will we, what CAN we talk about?

(*The sound of a train is heard. faintly at first then growing louder) DETTI waving at the train as it pulls out. MONI & ERIKA waving at DETTI as the sound of the train diminishes and then fades away.*)

(*MONI sits down next to ERIKA.*)

SCENE 9

MONI: (*After a long silence -- Lost*) Mutti, where are we going?

ERIKA: To Amerika -- your Papa is waiting for us there. Soon we will ALL be together again.

MONI: Is Amerika very far away?

ERIKA: Yes Monichen, it is far away.

MONI: You just said we would ALL be together again. (*angry*) You LIED! Detti is not with us. How can you say we will ALL be together again. THAT IS A LIE!

ERIKA: Be reasonable. I have explained to you that we are not safe staying. We must leave!

MONI: (*Increasingly more agitated throughout this speech.*) But I don't want to leave. I don't want to leave my home. This is where I belong. And I don't want to leave my Detti. She has always taken care of me.

How can I go to sleep without her being next to me? Why are we leaving her behind? Why can't she come with us to Amerika?

ERIKA: Because this is her home.

MONI: (*cries out*) But it is my home too! Why must we go? Why must I go?

ERIKA: You are too young to understand now. (*This is a promise.*) Some day you will.

MONI: No, I won't -- I will never understand -- I will always remember that Wien is my home, that this is where I belong -- this is my home!

(*Main Melody of :"WIEN, WIEN NUR DU ALLEIN" comes in slowly, plaintively -- everyone appears facing audience, as MONI's voice fades out they take up repeating "always remember."*)

I WILL NEVER FORGET, I WILL ALWAYS REMEMBER WIEN, ALWAYS REMEMBER DETTI, ALWAYS REMEMBER, ALWAYS REMEMBER, ALWAYS REMEMBER ....

POSTLUDE

ANNEMONE: Always remember ... There is so much I have forgotten. So many years ago. So many years ago when the future was an unknown. The future which is today the past and holds its own memories. Memories of much joy and of much sorrow,

(*Everyone except ANNEMONE backs off and slowly turns and exits stage leaving ANNEMONE alone on stage.*)

AND WHERE HAS ALL OF THIS REMEMBERING I PROMISED MYSELF, WHERE HAS THAT ALL VANISHED TO? WHERE? -- WHERE I WONDER?

(*Music continues. She turns upstage sees everyone has vanished and turns back to audience.*)

I WONDER?

(*Music up to a crescendo, then Music and Lights fade slowly.*)

(*Blackout as Music ends.*)

END OF PLAY

Dinner at the Steak Barn

by

Dean Glasel

Directed by Preston Boyd

with

Ted Mase as Husband
Nadia Watts as Wife
Angel Borths as Waitress
Jasmine McAllister as Hostess

CHARACTERS

WIFE (ANNE), a woman, in her thirties or forties
HUSBAND (HARRY), a man of like age
HOSTESS, a woman in her twenties
WAITRESS, a woman in her twenties

SETTING

Hostess stand in a restaurant.

TIME

Present day.

* * *

Lights up.

WIFE and HUSBAND wait at hostess stand.

WIFE: Alright, Harry, now that we're standing here waiting, be honest. Do you know anything about this restaurant, or is this another one of your wild guesses?

HUSBAND: From everything I hear, the food here is supposed to be great, so cut me a little slack, will you?

WIFE: God, I hope so. I'm just starving. We do have reservations, don't we? Please say we have reservations. You know how I hate waiting!

HUSBAND: Well, there's no problem there. I called and made them last week. Even got us a booth. Now, does that make you happy?

WIFE: Sounds great to me. But you must admit, your track record for getting us tables at good restaurants isn't very good!

HUSBAND: I promise you tonight will be different. I even called them back yesterday to confirm our reservation.

WIFE: I certainly hope the food here is better than the service. We've been waiting almost five minutes. I hope that's not an indication of how this place is run. Where is the Hostess, anyway?

HUSBAND: I don't know. I suppose she's off doing something.

WIFE: Off doing something, huh? Off doing something? Well, If I had known that, I would never have asked such a silly question. Thank you!

HUSBAND: Look, there are three things I don't know. One is the meaning of life, the second is who killed Jimmy Hoffa, and the other is where the Hostess is, OK?

WIFE: But we have reservations. She should be here. She knew that we would be here at 8:00 to get our table. I just don't understand why she's not here to seat us. This doesn't seem very professional to me.

HUSBAND: Anne, I reserved a table. I forgot to reserve the Hostess. Now, for god's sake, will you shut up!

WIFE: There's a Waitress over there. Go over and ask her. Maybe she can help us.

HUSBAND: (*crosses to WAITRESS, who is just entering*) Excuse me. Can you tell me where the Hostess is? We have reservations and we've been waiting for five minutes without seeing anyone.

WAITRESS: Gee, I don't know. She was here a while ago. She must have wandered off into the restaurant.

HUSBAND: Wandered off? You mean, like really wandered off?

WAITRESS: Uh huh.

HUSBAND: Well, I hope she dropped some bread crumbs so she can find her way back.

WAITRESS: Bread crumbs? Huh? Oh, I get it! Like in the fairy tales - those kind of bread crumbs. Hey, that's pretty funny!

HUSBAND: I'm glad I could amuse you. Now, will you please do me a favor and find someone who will seat us?

WAITRESS: Oh, I'm sure she'll be back any minute. Actually, I wanted to talk to her myself.

HUSBAND: Good, then. I hope for both our sakes she returns. If you don't mind, can I talk to her first. It would greatly benefit my blood pressure and my marriage! (*crosses back to his WIFE*)

WIFE: What did she say, Harry?

HUSBAND: Well, as best I can tell, she said the Hostess wandered off into the woods.

WIFE: What??!

HUSBAND: Never mind. You really had to be there!

HOSTESS: (*arriving at stand*) Hi! Welcome to the Steak Barn. May I help you?

HUSBAND: You did find your way back!

HOSTESS: What?

HUSBAND: Just a private joke between a waitress and myself. Anyhow, we have a reservation for a booth at 8:00. The name is ....

HOSTESS: (*answering cell phone*) Excuse me for a moment, please. (*giggly and sexy*) Well, hi! And how are you? What do you mean did I have a good time? How could I not have? Hey, listen, I can't really talk right now. Some people are standing here. Can I call you back? Bye - talk to you later. (*turning back to couple*) I'm sorry. Now, may I help you?

HUSBAND: Yes, we have a reservation for a booth at 8:00. The name is ...

WAITRESS: (*stops by*) I hear you went out with Bill last night. Word travels fast around here. Say, can I ask you a question? Everyone is sort of curious about one thing.

HOSTESS: Yes, I did. We really had a great time. Now, make it quick or ask me about it later. I've got some people here.

WAITRESS: If you don't mind me being personal, I hear he's really big, if you know what I mean. You don't have to say if you don't want to, but you hear these things and it sure makes you curious, as I said.

HOSTESS: Well, now don't say I said this, but you know that device that goes "beep, beep, beep" when heavy equipment backs up? Well, he needs one of those when he goes forward? I'll fill you in later at the party. (*WAITRESS giggles and leaves*) I'm sorry. Now, may I help you?

HUSBAND: I hate to admit it, but even I was getting curious. Anyhow, as I was saying before I inadvertently stumbled into an errant episode of "Days Of Our Lives," we have a reservation for a booth at 8:00. The name is ...

HOSTESS: Booth at 8:00. Oh, yes. I have it right here. Mr. (*phonetically*) SMUH-I-TITH, is it? Did I pronounce that correctly?

HOSTESS: Please excuse me. Now, where were we?

HUSBAND: You want to know where we were? I'll tell you where we were! You are standing in the same place you were standing when we met you, and we are standing in the same place we were standing when we came in, and we were coming here to eat, which so far, we haven't! That's where we were!

HOSTESS: Well, I should have something for you shortly. A lot of people are just about ready to leave. But you know how it is when people are in a restaurant. They just want to sit around and talk.

HUSBAND: You're right! If you've already eaten, it's fun! But when you're waiting for a table, this hanging around talking thing loses something!

WIFE: Excuse me. I certainly don't want to hold us up, but have I got time to go to the ladies room before our booth is ready?

HOSTESS: Oh, I think so. In fact, you've probably got enough time to not only go number one, but also number two, if you have to.

HUSBAND: What!!!!!???

HOSTESS: I was only trying to say that we have plenty of time and she doesn't need to hurry. I certainly didn't mean anything by it!

HUSBAND: Stay here, Anne! You can go after we're seated. Now, look. Do you have a booth for us or not? What's the purpose of making a reservation if when you get here, there's no place to sit? I thought that's why people make reservations. But then I thought you came to restaurants to eat, not to bond with the employees!

HOSTESS: If you'll wait just a moment, I'll go see what we have. (*leaves for about 30 seconds*)

WIFE: Harry, I thought you said you made reservations!

HUSBAND: Don't go there, Anne! Don't go there!

HOSTESS: Now, the good news is we do have a booth, but the bad news is we can't get the bus boys to clean it. It's a problem we have from time to time. We can't always get them to understand what we're saying. I don't suppose either of you speaks Spanish, do you?

HUSBAND: SMUH-I-TITH? Let me see that. It must be spelled wrong. No, no - it's spelled correctly. But I've never heard it pronounced that way before. In fact, I've never heard it mispronounced at all! Ever!

HOSTESS: I'm so sorry. What is the correct pronunciation?

HUSBAND: Smith! That's how it's pronounced. Smith! Trust me!

HOSTESS: Oh! That's one of those names that's pronounced differently than it's spelled.

HUSBAND: Right! yeah! It must be the fact that it only has one "m" in it that threw you!

WAITRESS: (*comes up again*) Hey, let me see the floor plan for a second. Whoa! Wait a minute! You'd better not seat anyone else in Section 6 - the new guy's station. He is really in the weeds! Why he's scheduled on a busy night, I'll never understand!

HOSTESS: You know, that's really funny! I had a friend of mine who worked with him over at Bongo Burger who told me he would tank if he had more than two tables.

WAITRESS: I tried to tell Steve not to hire him, but you know Steve! No matter what I say, he just won't listen to me. I don't know what the problem is! I've been here a long time and he knows I know what I'm talking about!

HOSTESS: I think the problem is you won't go to bed with him! C'mon! How bad can he be?

WAITRESS: I tell you what - you go to bed with him! I think he smells like French fries!

HOSTESS: (*cell phone rings again - she answers*) (*aside to HUSBAND and WIFE*) Excuse me. I'll be right with you. Hi. No, we're all meeting at Kathy's later after work and, listen, if you want to smoke, you've got to bring your own stuff. OK, well, I've got an extra bag I can sell you. Hopefullly, we can get these people out of here by ten or ten-thirty. Alright. I'll see you there.

HOSTESS: I'm sorry. We're just having a very busy night.

HUSBAND: No, you're wrong. The restaurant isn't having a busy night. YOU are having a busy night!

WIFE: Well, I did take one semester in high school,, and in college our sorority went to Mexico for spring break, but I'm not sure how ...

HUSBAND: Anne, will you shut up!

WIFE: Don't yell at me! I was only trying to help! I didn't see you offering any suggestions!

HUSBAND: Frankly, I didn't think the fact that I like tacos and refried beans qualified me to solve the situation!

WIFE: No, but I could tell you what it DOES qualify you to do, and you have done it on far too many occasions! (*HUSBAND glares at her.*)

HUSBAND: Look, all we wanted was to have a nice, quiet, romantic dinner. If you don't have a booth, we'll take a table. At this point, eating is more important than where we sit. So just seat us anywhere, assuming the restaurant is still open and everyone hasn't left for Kathy's!

HOSTESS: Well, if you'll wait another moment, I'll go see if we have a table available. Something should have freed up by now. (*leaves*)

WIFE: Harry, I hate to bring this reservation thing up again, but it seems to me that ...

HUSBAND: Anne, if you don't shut up, we're only going to need a reservation for one! Then you can talk to Juan and Jose about your impressions of Mexico while they are bussing tables! Because I won't be there!

HOSTESS: (*returns*) Well, as it happens, we do have an available table, but it's a six top and we're not supposed to seat less than five. If you'd like, there's a party of three over there that's been waiting for a while, and I'd be glad to seat all of you together immediately.

HUSBAND: That's it! That's it! We've been standing here god knows how long, and in that time, though we've not been seated, we've been privy to some interesting insights and occurrences. For instance, we know that your date last night, Bill, by all accounts is well-endowed, or should I say "Beep, Beep, Beep"? My last name, one of the simplest and most common in the entire United States of America was mauled and mangled. I learned that the new waiter who was hired from Bongo Burger shouldn't have been hired from Bongo Burger and wouldn't have been hired from Bongo Burger had the waitress who helped you avert a crises in Section Six, slept with Steve, the Manager of The Steak Barn, and, further, it became apparent that this restaurant not only depends on bilingual customers to get its tables bussed, but it also depends on its customers to eat dinner with strangers so as to not violate the House's seating policies. But the real icing on the cake, if you'll forgive me mentioning food in a restaurant where it seems impossible to get any, is that some young ditz whose bra size is bigger than her IQ gave my wife permission to go to the ladies room to do either Number One or Number Two, or a combination of both, her choice, of course! As far as I'm concerned, this whole restaurant is full of Number Two!

HOSTESS: I'm sorry, sir, that you seem to be unhappy with your Steak Barn experience. Our customers are always very important to us, and the last thing Steak Barn wants is for any of them to be unhappy.

HUSBAND: Unhappy?! Unhappy!? I'll show you unhappy! (*Starts to lunge for HOSTESS. WIFE restrains him.*)

WIFE: Harry! Harry! Calm down!

HUSBAND: Let's get out of here while I still have some semblence of self control! (WIFE and HUSBAND turn and walk toward door.) Oh, and by the way, we won't be at Kathy's, unless, of course, she will be serving hor d'oeuvres, and it will be easier to get into than this place!

HOSTESS: Sir, if you'd like, I can let you speak to the Manager.

HUSBAND: (*turns back to HOSTESS*) You mean Steve? No thanks! I hear he smells like French fries! (*They then pass WAITRESS standing at the door.*)

WAITRESS: Goodnight! We hope you enjoyed your Steak Barn experience. Please come see us again! (HUSBAND breaks away and charges towards the WAITRESS.)

HUSBAND: See you again?!!!! Why I'll.........

WIFE: (excitedly) Harry, NO!!!! (drags him offstage)

HOSTESS: (*when WIFE and HUSBAND are gone*) Smith, party of two. Your table is ready. Smith.....

(*Blackout*)

END OF PLAY

Necessary Evil

by

Michael Phelan

Directed by Louise Stinespring, Ph.D.

with

Cael Barkman as Lucy
Tom Aposporos as Michael

CHARACTERS

LUCY, a female of any age
MICHAEL, a male or female of any age

SETTING

An office area or waiting area with a small table and two chairs.

TIME

Before creation.

* * *

Lights up.

LUCY and MICHAEL enter, with LUCY leading. LUCY is direct and expressive, dressed in a sharp business suit. MICHAEL is quieter, earnest, and is dressed somewhat more casually.

LUCY: He's lost it. I'm telling you, this time he's lost it.

MICHAEL: It is quite a project.

LUCY: What could he possibly be thinking? This is beyond reasonable.

MICHAEL: And he wants it all done in seven days.

LUCY: Six days, Michael. Didn't you hear? He wants it done in six days.

MICHAEL: True. And on the seventh day ...

LUCY: You want to put rings around Saturn, that's one thing. Canals on Mars, that's another.

MICHAEL: At least it's not as big as Jupiter was.

LUCY: And what an ugly name. "Earth." It sounds like a burp. What, did he run out of names all of a sudden? Jupiter, now there's a name. Venus, Neptune, Mars, those are names.

MICHAEL: I don't think "Earth" is all that bad.

LUCY: A billion different species. Two of every kind, male and female. Plants. Animals.

MICHAEL: What's a plant?

LUCY: What's an animal!

MICHAEL: Man. Wo-man.

LUCY: This is not a project, it's a fiasco. What do you think? Don't you think he's gone too far this time?

MICHAEL: I don't think he'd give us anything we couldn't handle, Lucy.

LUCY: In six days? You can't do all this in six days. It defies the laws of physics.

MICHAEL: But he wrote the laws of physics. If he wrote them, he can un-write them, can't he?

LUCY: No, because he said they were immutable.

MICHAEL: Well, after all, he is God.

LUCY: God is not supposed to change his mind.

MICHAEL: You'd better not let him hear you talking like this.

LUCY: Let him hear. Hey, God! You hear me?

MICHAEL: Sssshh! Lucy! You want to get us in trouble?

LUCY: You know what I think? I think we ought to go back in there.

MICHAEL: And try to reason with him?

LUCY: No ... I'm thinking it's time for a change in leadership.

MICHAEL: You want to overthrow God.

LUCY: Not "overthrow" him. Just -- ask him to step aside, that's all.

MICHAEL: But I love God.

LUCY: I didn't say you can't love him. Just help me take him out.

MICHAEL: But Lucy, he made us.

LUCY: So? That's not my fault. Michael, listen to me. God is not what he used to be. But you and me, we're strong. We're vital! We could run this place like a well-oiled machine.

MICHAEL: Our job is to do what he says. Just because you're on some power trip, is no reason to mutiny against God. Where's your sense of duty, Lucy?

LUCY: Oh, spare me. Duty. What is that, anyway?

MICHAEL: It's what we're supposed to do, is what it is. Didn't he teach you anything?

LUCY: You need to open your mind, Michael. Think of the possibilities. You call it duty? I call it slavery. You call it mutiny? I call it opportunity.

MICHAEL: You are really scaring me, Lucy. No one has ever said "no" to God before.

LUCY: No one has ever had the guts, that's why. He's had his time, now it's our turn. You know what? I'm going in there.

MICHAEL: No!

LUCY: Get out of my way, Michael.

MICHAEL: I won't let you do this to him.

LUCY: Michael. Sit down for a moment. Please.

(*They sit.*)

Sweetie, you've got me all wrong. I love God just as much as you do. But look at it this way. This "Earth" project is lunacy. You know it as well as I do. It can't be done, not the way he wants it.

MICHAEL: How do you know, if we don't try?

LUCY: Now, I can understand your loyalty. I really can. And I respect it, honestly I do.

MICHAEL: But?

LUCY: But nothing. You're honest, and trustworthy, and true blue straight as an arrow. And I admire you for that, I really do. Now, being who we are, we have a lot of responsibility on our shoulders. The well-being of the entire universe: it rests with us, right?

MICHAEL: And with God.

LUCY: Of course. So. If something were to come along and jeopardize that well-being, that would be a pretty serious thing, wouldn't you say?

MICHAEL: Where is this going, Lucy?

LUCY: Michael, honestly, I'm on your side. All I'm saying is: if some mistaken idea or lapse in judgment were to threaten everything we've worked so hard to create, don't you think we ought to try our best to prevent it from happening?

MICHAEL: If that were to happen, yes. As long as it's okay with God.

LUCY: Exactly. Now, I'm the last angel in Heaven to want to hurt God. I love God! Just like you. I just think we need to help him see things for what they are, that's all. Maybe he needs to cut back his workload. Let someone else run things for awhile.

MICHAEL: Like you.

LUCY: And you.

MICHAEL: And what about God?

LUCY: We let him rest. We keep him in the dark. Let him worry about other things, or better yet, not worry at all.

MICHAEL: I still don't like it.

LUCY: You don't trust me. Well, isn't that rich! Here I am, trying to take a nice, rational approach, and you don't trust me. Haven't we worked side by side for billions of years? Stuck by each other through thick and thin?

MICHAEL: But you're talking about -- I don't know, blasphemy. You're talking about upsetting the balance.

LUCY: Balance is exactly what I'm talking about! Don't you get it? Look at this place. Lots of little angels, good little angels, all wandering around in perfect precision: "Yes, God," "Right away, God," "Anything else, God?" That's not balance. Balance has two sides.

MICHAEL: But it's stable. Stability gives you something to count on.

LUCY: Well, you know what? I'm sick of it. And I'm sick of taking orders. And I'm saying, let's do something about it. Now are you in, or are you out?

(*A bell is heard: two rings.*)

MICHAEL: Two rings. That means you.

LUCY: Well. Perfect timing.

MICHAEL: I wonder if he overheard you.

LUCY: Well, so what? I'm not afraid. I hope he did hear. It'll cushion the blow. So, are you coming with me?

MICHAEL: I don't think so.

LUCY: I thought we were a team.

MICHAEL: If you're going to tell God he's fired, you're on your own.

LUCY: Alright, fine. But I'll remember this, Michael. You had your chance. All the things we did, and all the projects we pulled off ... and this is what it all comes down to. Well, right now you're nothing to me but a traitor. You hear me? A traitor! You'll be working on black holes, when I get through with you.

(*Two more rings*)

I'm coming!

(*LUCY exits. MICHAEL paces for a moment, then pauses ... then approaches the exit cautiously and attempts to listen for a moment, but thinks better of it and crosses to center and prays.*)

MICHAEL: Lord, please go easy on Lucy. She doesn't really know what she's saying. She's under a lot of stress right now, and I think it's kind of getting to her. But she'll be okay. She's a good angel, Lord, and I know she means well. She just has a strange way of showing it sometimes. But we couldn't have done Jupiter without her. And no one else could figure out how to do the rings around Saturn -- but in the end, she was the one that made it happen. And they're beautiful. The sun, the Milky Way ... we couldn't have done any of that without her. So leave it to me. Just let me work with her awhile, and in a couple of days she'll be her old self again. We'll get this Earth thing done, and you'll be proud of her. I promise. I remain your most humble servant, Lord. Amen.

(*LUCY enters proudly, carrying a business card.*)

LUCY: Well. Aren't you going to congratulate me?

MICHAEL: On what?

LUCY: He saw things exactly my way.

MICHAEL: You're kidding.

LUCY: Not at all. As a matter of fact, I'm "leaving to pursue other career opportunities outside the organization." I made that up myself, you know.

MICHAEL: Where are you going?

LUCY: I get to create a parallel world, all by myself. It's exactly the chance I've been waiting for. See? I even get a name change.

(*She shows the business card to MICHAEL.*)

MICHAEL: Satin.

LUCY: Long "A".

MICHAEL: Satan?

LUCY: Has a nice ring, doesn't it? Sounds ... ominous. Dangerous. No more "Lucifer" for this little angel.

MICHAEL: Well, congratulations, I guess. When do you start?

LUCY: ASAP.

MICHAEL: Wow. Good for you. I'm sure going to miss you, though.

LUCY: Don't. This is exactly the chance I've been waiting for. I can see it now. A silent black river. A grand entranceway. Huge pillars of fire on either side, an enormous gilded sign overhead: "Abandon all hope, ye who enter here." I love it. See what happens when you have the guts to speak your mind? See you 'round, sucker.

(*Exits, laughing*)

(*Blackout*)

END OF PLAY

Shared Sorrow

by

M. John Bohane

Directed by Pam Wiley

with

Richard Pell as Tom
William Muzzillo as Peter

CHARACTERS

TOM, a widower in his seventies
PETER, a widower in his seventies

SETTING

The sitting room in Tom's house.

TIME

The present, late one night.

* * *

Lights up.

Two chairs and a coffee table. An old sick looking man, TOM, sits alone in his living room. A half-finished glass of red wine stands on a coffee table in front of him. He stares at the glass. After a while he turns towards the kitchen.

TOM: (*shouting*) Found it yet?

PETER: (*shouting back from kitchen*) Where the hell do you keep the ice?

TOM: In the freezer. Where else?

PETER: There's none in the freezer.

TOM: (*to himself*) Shit! (*shouting to PETER*) Sorry. I forgot. The ice-maker doesn't work.

(*TOM goes back to staring at his glass as PETER comes into the room carrying a glass of whiskey.*)

PETER: Jesus, Tom. You're letting the place fall apart. There's nothing left in the fridge.

(*TOM does not reply. PETER sits on the chair next to TOM and takes a long drink from his glass.*)

PETER: (*continuing, putting the glass on the table*) Nice whiskey. (*pause*) Would have liked some ice with it, though.

TOM: (*angrily*) Shit! Peter. If that's all you've got to worry about ... I'm sorry! Sorry.

PETER: You okay?

TOM: Yeah. I'm fine.

PETER: You don't look so good.

TOM: Getting old, Peter. Getting old.

PETER: Aren't we all? (*pause*) Why did you call? We haven't seen each other since ... well, since a while ago. I was wondering if something was wrong.

TOM: Wrong? No. Nothing's wrong. (*pause*) Just wanted ... some company.

PETER: That's good, Tom. That's good. It's been some time since ... since Anne passed away.

(*silence*)

PETER: (*continuing*) So, what have you been up to?

TOM: Nothing much. Thinking, mainly.

PETER: Was it Shakespeare who wrote, "He thinks too much: such men are dangerous?"

(*silence*)

PETER: (*continuing*) How long has it been now, since Anne ... passed away.

TOM: For Christ's sake, stop saying 'passed away'. She died. She just ... died.

PETER: I use "passed away" because she's gone onto another world. A better one.

TOM: When you die, you die.

PETER: Let's not get into another one of those arguments.

TOM: You're right. It's too late.

PETER: Too late?

(*silence*)

PETER: (*continuing*) How long have we known each other?

TOM: Don't you know?

PETER: Come on, Tom! Snap out of it. You're in a shitty mood.

TOM: Sorry! Sorry.

PETER: Will you stop saying, "sorry!"

TOM: Sorry ... ah ... sorry. Shit!

(*silence*)

PETER: Fifty years.

TOM: "Fifty years" what?

PETER: We've know each other fifty years.

TOM: Jesus, where did it all go?

(*silence*)

TOM: (*continuing*) I killed her, you know.

PETER: You what?

TOM: Anne. I killed her.

PETER: You can't blame yourself, Tom. I know you didn't have much of a relationship but you can't blame yourself for her death. She died of cancer.

TOM: It was all too much in the end. Watching her in agony day after day. The drugs hardly worked anymore. So I killed her.

PETER: You don't know what you're saying.

TOM: Waited for the nurse to leave the room and then pulled the pillow down over her face. Held it there forever, it seemed. Until I heard the nurse returning. I pretended to be asleep on the couch next to her bed.

PETER: Dear God!

(*silence*)

PETER: (*continuing*) Why are you telling me this now?

TOM: It's time.

PETER: Time for what?

TOM: Time to ... to make amends.

(*TOM suddenly sits up.*)

TOM: (*continuing*) Why did you do it?

PETER: Do what?

TOM: You and Anne. Why did you do it?

PETER: You've lost me.

TOM: She told me about the two of you.

(*silence*)

TOM: (*continuing*) Come on, Peter. I need to know.

(*silence*)

TOM: (*continuing, struggling to get up from his chair*) For fuck's sake, tell me!

(*TOM has a coughing fit. PETER jumps up and helps TOM to sit back into his chair.*)

PETER: (*sitting*) She was lonely. You and she hadn't spoken for months. She just wanted someone ... someone to talk to.

TOM: It was more than talk, wasn't it?

PETER: Tom, it was nothing really. Just two lonely souls reaching out.

TOM: I was going to kill you.

PETER: What?

TOM: Poison.

PETER: Poison?

TOM: In your drink. I bought it yesterday.
(*PETER jumps up from his chair.*)

PETER: Jesus!

TOM: Don't worry. Decided against it.

(*PETER slowly sits down.*)

PETER: Christ, Tom, you nearly gave me a heart attack.

TOM: That would have been a laugh, wouldn't it?

PETER: It's no laughing matter.

(*silence*)

PETER: (*continuing*) What do we do now?

TOM: Nothing. Just wanted someone to be here.

(*silence*)

PETER: Can I get you more wine?

TOM: No. No. I think I've had enough. It should be working by now.

PETER: Working?

TOM: I put it in the wine.

PETER: You put poison in the wine?

TOM: Seemed to be the easiest thing to do.

PETER: (*jumping up*) Jesus, Tom. I'll call a doctor.

TOM: Too late for that.

PETER: (*sitting*) Why did you do it?

TOM: I took the poison because ... well, because I want to be with her.

PETER: I thought you didn't believe in any of that?

TOM: No atheists in foxholes, you know.

(*silence*)

PETER: I'm sorry, Tom.

TOM: At least you gave her some joy. I just took away the pain.

PETER: I mean, I'm sorry about ... everything. (*pause*) Ever since Joan passed away I've wondered myself if it's really worth going on.

(*PETER stands and paces around the room not noticing that TOM is slowly closing his eyes.*)

PETER: (*continuing*) The burden of getting out of bed. Dragging my tired body through each empty day. Ending every evening lost in a hazy mist of alcohol. You know what I mean.

(*PETER does not realize TOM has died.*)

PETER: (continuing) Loneliness seeps into your soul like a cancer. There's just no joy left in life any more. It really makes no sense to keep--

(*PETER looks at TOM.*)

PETER: (*continuing*) Jesus, Tom! You've got me all depressed. (*pause*) Tom? Tom!

(*PETER realizes TOM is dead and checks his pulse. He picks up his glass of whiskey, studies it for a moment, and then puts it back on the table. He stares at TOM's glass of wine and slowly picks it up. He raises the glass to give a toast to TOM.*)

PETER: (*continuing*) Fifty years, my old friend. Fifty years. A lifetime. (*pause*) Bottoms up!

(*PETER starts drinking the wine.*)

(*Blackout*)

END OF PLAY

The Mermaid's Secret

by

Janis R. Frawley

Directed by Fred Zimmerman

with

Karle H. Murdock as Jessica
David Abolafia as Kyle
CHARACTERS

JESSICA, a 40-50ish, playful, light-hearted, carefree, artsy female spirit, dressed in a colorful gypsy/hippie style. Her hair is long, and free-flowing. She's a creative, confident woman who is comfortable with who she is.
KYLE, a 45-50ish man, short hair, clean shaven, fit-n-trim, dressed extremely conservatively in black dress pants, designer loafers, white long-sleeved shirt. He's stiff and stuffy, with the look of an Evangelist.

SETTING

In the close quarters of an attic.

TIME

Late 1980's -early 1990's.

* * *

Lights up.

Memorabilia of a life together surrounds JESSICA and KYLE. Feather boas hang from hooks, fishing poles, skis, a pretty long-fringed shawl is draped over an old rocking chair, peace and love posters, etc. Artist supplies (easels, canvases, color-stained palettes) are also scattered amidst the memorabilia. Jessica is sitting on the floor rummaging through an old trunk.

JESSICA: I just love the junk in this old trunk. (*Picks up an ornate hash pipe and putting it up to her lips, pretending to take a toke.*) Every piece pulses with that electric energy of the sixties! (*Examines it more closely.*) Oh, look! There's still some little pieces of hashish in the bowl. (*Holds it up to her nose and takes a long whiff.*) Mmmmm! Aromatherapy at its best. You know, I think I hid a special little box in here years ago ... (*Starts digging around in the chest.*)

KYLE: Oh, Lord, deliver me from this for I am not in the mood to relive our early days. All I want is my family heirlooms and to get this damned divorce over.

JESSICA: (*Ignoring him as she digs around in the chest and comes up with a pretty box.*) Ah! Here it is. (*Takes the lid off and takes out a pack of matches and a baggie with some hashish in it.*) I had stashed this away for a stormy day. Looks like it's arrived with blustery vibes. I wonder if this stuff is still any good. (*Carefully puts some hashish in the pipe and lights it.*)

KYLE: The devil's got hold of you, Jessica, luring you down an evil path. You know that despicable stuff is against the law ... and it's against everything I stand for now.

JESSICA: You used to love getting high! (*Takes a toke on the pipe.*) Boy, we did some wild and crazy shit back then, didn't we? It was so ... gloriously exhilarating!

KYLE: Put it away, Jessica. I'd hate to get hauled off to jail at this stage of my life. My career, my reputation, would all go straight down to Hades.

JESSICA: (*Takes another toke and offers it to KYLE, who brushes it away with his hand.*) Ah, you never used to care if we got busted. Remember when ...

KYLE: I'm not proud of the stunts I pulled back then, but I've sought God's forgiveness. If my church ever found out half the stuff I used to do, they'd kick me out faster than you could say Jesus, Mary, and Joseph. They'd think I was possessed by the devil and that would mean the end of my business.

JESSICA: Oh, screw your church and your business! You were at your best back then. Free-thinking, spontaneous, independent ... creative beyond belief! I don't even know who you are anymore, quoting the Bible, talking about Jesus all of the time ... and dressing up like some freaking undertaker. (*She looks at him as if she's sizing him up, then re-lights the pipe and takes a hit.*) I know you've got religion, honey, but damn, you've lost your soul!

KYLE: I've saved my soul, Jessica.

JESSICA: Saved it from what? Me?

KYLE: Well, ...

JESSICA: (*ignoring him*) From a little hash? A bit of fun? Lighten up, Kyle. (*pause*) You know, some say Jesus was a hippie.

KYLE: That's blasphemy, Jessica! Jesus was the son of God.

JESSICA: (*Takes a hit off the pipe.*) So are you, KYLE ... and I'm his daughter.

KYLE: Your irreverence turns my stomach!

JESSICA: (*offering him the pipe*) Here. This does wonders for nausea.

KYLE: Isn't it time you grew up?

JESSICA: Like you did?

KYLE: One of us had to.

JESSICA: (*shoots him a dirty look*) You didn't grow up ... you grew old.

KYLE: A man has to get serious at some point in his life. So does a woman, I might add. By the way, aren't you getting a little too old to dress -- and act -- like a flitter-brained flower child?

JESSICA: The way I dress used to set your magic twanger hummin', darlin'.

KYLE: Don't even go there!

JESSICA: Oh, hell, Kyle, I'll wear whatever tickles my spirit, no matter what my age. I'm into authentic living ... staying true to myself, unlike someone else I know.

KYLE: Authentic? As in honest and forthright? What a pathetic joke!

JESSICA: What the hell does that mean? (*Ignoring him, she takes another toke and offers it to Kyle, who continues to refuse it.*) Man, I haven't puffed on a pipe in years! I wish you'd take a hit .... It would help make the evening, well, ... more pleasant ... for both of us. Maybe it would loosen you up enough to get back to being the great artist you were meant to be.

KYLE: You're not going to lead me into temptation this day, or any other day. And I won't talk about my art, especially with you!

JESSICA: The art world was touting you as America's next great star ... then greed and God ambushed you.

KYLE: Leave my God out of this. (*somberly*) I was just tired, Jessica, tired of being a starving artist, worn down by living off my wife. If you define greed as simply working hard to take care of my family, then so be it.

JESSICA: You sold out.

KYLE: A man's role is to protect his marriage. Each man has to do what he must to keep his self-respect, like providing his wife with what she needs ... and wants. Sure, I faked the religion at first to get customers into the book shop, but then Jesus touched me in a very real way. He filled an empty hole that just kept growing deeper and darker. You never understood any of it.

JESSICA; You were born to give great art to the world. I was glad to keep us afloat while you painted.

KYLE: Were you, now?

JESSICA: Why would you even question that? I was your most devoted groupie.

KYLE: Benefactor, you mean.

JESSICA: Major collectors were beginning to notice your work, and you just up and ...

KYLE: I couldn't take the ridicule any more. Even my old man called me a gigolo. There's no pride in being a kept man, Jessica.

JESSICA: The guy I married could've cared less about what others thought. He had faith in himself ... and in us. We had a grand plan for our life together and you just blew it off!

KYLE: Circumstances change a man.

JESSICA: Change! That's an understatement! Now you're so damned tight assed you can hardly breathe. (*Takes another toke, shows signs of getting higher, and offers the pipe to him again.*) Here ... take it for, God's sake. It's the mental enema you need. Maybe it'll revive that wild and crazy side of you that I fell in love with.

KYLE: It's against the law, Jessica. You know that goes against ...

JESSICA: (*mockingly*) ... everything you stand for now. (*Undisturbed, she goes back to rooting around in the chest.*) Oh, look at these old albums! Far out – Santana! (*Starts laughing and pulls out a wild vintage outfit, complete with a 50's style hat.*) Remember when I went to the vintage clothing store and bought this "Go Rock Rock" outfit?

KYLE: (*as if he were bored*) Yeah, I remember.

JESSICA: (*Holding it up in front of her, dancing and flirting, while singing a little of Santana's "Go Rock, Rock".*) When I'd put this on and groove to the music, you'd get hotter than a habanero pepper! You'd strip me in less than four seconds, lift me up on the dining room table, and let pure passion and pleasure rule the night. Then you'd grab your brushes and paint like a madman 'til dawn. Aahh! Those were magical times.

KYLE: (*Guarding himself from being caught up in the moment*) I'd rather not resurrect dead memories.

JESSICA: (*Taking another hit and ignoring him.*) We were magnificent! Love, peace and happiness was our religion! You were your own man back then.

KYLE: I'm not my own man, now?

JESSICA: The church owns you now.

KYLE: That's better than you owning me!

JESSICA: Kyle, I never ....

KYLE: (*sarcastically*) Nick said you did. Yeah, my frigging brother, who told me I had no backbone, no brains ... no talent ... that I wasn't good enough for you because I was a lazy, shiftless bum! He christened me a pariah because I was feeding off my wife just to make my own dreams come true.

JESSICA: I wish you hadn't bought into all of that. You were twenty times the man he ever was.

KYLE: In whose eyes?

JESSICA: In mine, of course ... until you packed away your brushes and canvases and headed down mainstream USA, preaching scripture every second of the day. (*Takes another toke.*)

KYLE: It wouldn't hurt you to live by the ten commandments once in a while.

JESSICA: (*Offers him the pipe again. He brushes her off with a swift flick of his hand.*) Kyle, honey, there is no commandment that says, "thou shalt not get high on hash." God placed it on earth to help mankind lighten up a bit.

KYLE: What about the one that says, Thou shalt not covet thy husband's brother.

JESSICA: It's thou shalt not covet thy neighbor's ... (*She stops and looks at Kyle in a strange way.*)

KYLE: I know, Jessica.

JESSICA: What are you talking about?

KYLE: Your affair with my brother.

JESSICA: (*Puts the pipe down, and laughs nervously.*) Good God, Kyle, Satan is playing games with your head.

KYLE: You've been playing games with my head ... for about twenty agonizing years!

JESSICA: No, I haven't . I ....

KYLE: ... prosperous, successful Nick, always putting down his little brother who had loads of talent but no money to give his wife a lot of pretty baubles. I didn't think any of that mattered to you, but, Nick, it seems, knew you a lot better than I did. (*becoming more angry*) May you both go straight to hell!

JESSICA: Kyle, I never ...

KYLE: (*so angry he's ready to pop a vein*) God damn it, cut the crap, Jessica!

JESSICA: Kyle, you never use the Lord's name in vein. It's against everything ...

KYLE: You just couldn't resist him, could you? His classy suits, expensive cars, and that irresistible charm that always gets him everything he wants in life ... including his brother's wife. I can see it now ... the two of you pretending to meet because you both were so worried that poor ol' Kyle was an artist gone mad.

JESSICA: We were worried. You had become obsessed...

KYLE: My best work came out of that time.

JESSICA: I know, but ...

KYLE: (*anger mounting*) ... but then the chemistry sparked between you and Nick, while you were sipping champagne and sharing chateaubriand in fancy restaurants bathed in candlelight. And we can't forget those seductive hotel suites where he bedded you while I was home, in my own little dream world ... painting my life away. Poor, blind Kyle, ... painting, always painting ... never realizing I had my own beloved Judas lying beside me most every night, betraying the sacredness of our vows and our love ... the liar who never really believed in that grand plan that you always accuse me of blowing off!

JESSICA: OK! OK! I was working my ass off in two jobs that I hated! I'd come home and there you'd be, in the same pajamas I left you in that morning. You never even combed your hair ... dirty dishes and empty bottles of cheap Chianti were piled in the sink. Night after night I'd come home to this mess ... I deserved more ...

KYLE: (*very angry*) Well, baby, exhausted, or not, you perfectly played the role of supportive wife. YOU were the one who kept telling me to stay home and paint. You and your pretense make me sick.

JESSICA: (*on the verge of tears*) I needed a man who ...

KYLE: My brother, for Christ's sake? Do you know how God damned sick that is?

JESSICA: Kyle!

KYLE: (*very sarcastically*) Forgive me if I offended you, your freaking highness.

JESSICA: Oh, Kyle, I was exhausted, and so confused, and Nick ... If only you could've started making some real money on your paintings.

KYLE: (*hesitating a moment*) I did. An Italian collector bought one for $85,000.

JESSICA: $85,000! You never told me ...

KYLE: There was no reason to. He bought it right after I buried my brushes in that trunk and swore never to paint again. (*Walks toward the trunk and starts searching for his painter's box.*) It was two days after I found out that my loving, supportive wife was bopping the be-

Jesus out of my brother. I've both hated - and loved - you from that moment on.

JESSICA: Which painting?

KYLE: (*Pulling his painter's box out of the trunk, he slowly opens it and, takes out his paint brushes, intently feeling each one, as if for the first time.*) The Mermaid.

JESSICA: I posed hours for that painting ...

KYLE: (*reminiscingly*) With seashells and glitter woven through your long, beautiful hair.

JESSICA: And every moment felt as if you were making love to me with your eyes.

KYLE: Yea, you were the goddess that I worshipped back then ... the one I had mistakenly put all of my faith in. (*Carefully puts the brushes back in the box and closes it.*) But that's all over, Jessica. The secret is finally out. The burden has been lifted, and for the first time in what seems like a lifetime, I can breathe. I am finally free. (*Puts the box under his arm and exits without looking back.*)

JESSICA: (*Falls to her knees and wraps her arms around herself.*) Lord, forgive me for I knew not what I did. I implore you ... show me the way to hold on to the only man I have truly ever loved.

(*Blackout*)

END OF PLAY

Underneath

by

Connie Schindewolf

Directed by Pam Wiley

with

Laurie Zimmerman as Florence
Laine Forman as Sarah

CHARACTERS

FLORENCE, A woman in her early fifties who is recovering from a broken ankle. She's led somewhat of a sheltered life being in her husband's shadow. Now he's dead. When she's passionate about something, she becomes quite vibrant.

SARAH, A young woman in her twenties, concerned about her mother since the death of her father. Her own marriage is faltering and she's finding motherhood trying.

SETTING

Florence's deck on the back of her house overlooking the bay.

TIME

The present.

* * *

Lights up.

There is a table with three chairs, center. FLORENCE is sitting at the table working on her laptop. Crutches are to her side. She is dependent on her crutches when walking in the first half of the play and then becomes increasingly less dependent on them until she finally does not use them at all but walks with a limp.

Sarah enters, carrying some papers and approaches stage right side of table.

SARAH: Mom, I knew you'd be out here.

FLORENCE: (*closing her laptop*) Hi Babe!

(*Sarah bends and artificially hugs her mother.*)

SARAH: How are you Mom? Ankle hurt?

FLORENCE: You know, once I got that cast off and could scratch those itches that have been driving me up the wall, I knew I'd live.

SARAH: But you're not supposed to walk yet are you? I mean, without the crutches?

FLORENCE: The Doctor said I could slowly start putting weight on it and by next week throw these things away. But you didn't come here to ask me about my ankle. You gave me your let's-check-on-poor-old-Mom call yesterday.

SARAH: Mom, since Daddy died I worry about you, that's all.

FLORENCE: Uh huh. So what are the papers?

SARAH: Mom, we've got to talk about the property.

FLORENCE: Would you like some lemonade? Made with Sweet & Low, very low cal and lots of vitamin C?

SARAH: No thanks, I just stopped at Starbucks, so if I seem wired, that latte is to blame. (*pause*) Mom, they've called me about the contract.

FLORENCE: Sarah this is not your problem. Let me handle this.

SARAH: Mom, I promised Daddy I would help you with things like this. $500,000 Mom. Do you know what you can buy with that?

FLORENCE: Did Harold send you that? That old curmudgeon! He would have to get you involved. I'm not signing!

SARAH: He's just representing the homeowner's association, Mom. Everyone has agreed to sell but you. These houses are 40 years old—they don't meet hurricane codes, and being right on the bay, you're very vulnerable. Just put "Florence Davis" right there and it's done.

FLORENCE: (*looking out at the water*) You know I saw a loon out there yesterday—it reminded me of On Golden Pond. Sarah, do you remember when we watched that together, you, me, and your father?

SARAH: I know you love this old house ... and it has so many memories for you.

FLORENCE: It's not the house. (*pause*) It's what's underneath.

SARAH: What do you mean "underneath"? (*Florence doesn't respond.*) I know it makes you sick to think of condos here, but Mom, you may never get more than $500,000. You could buy a nice three-bedroom condo on the mainland for that.

FLORENCE: Why on earth would I need three bedrooms? (*no answer*) There's something more here, Sarah. Why are you interfering?

SARAH: Mom, Daddy would want me to take care of you!

FLORENCE: I'm not in the grave yet. So I tripped in a hole in the yard and broke my ankle. I'm not exactly nursing home material for God's sakes—I'm only in my 50's!

SARAH: (*pause*) What did you mean by something underneath this house?

FLORENCE: Forget it Sarah, you wouldn't understand. Nor would any of my neighbors who used to be my friends. They just want me to sign those papers so they can get their $500,000 and get out of here. I'm just an incidental take.

SARAH: What?

FLORENCE: Never mind. I'm sorry they involved you, Sarah. Go home.

SARAH: OH MY GOD! This has something to do with Daddy, doesn't it? Underneath? Did he bury something before he built the deck? Mom, did he kill something, or ... someone?

FLORENCE: For God's sake Sarah, calm down. Your father had a temper yes, but kill someone? You really didn't know him very well if you think that.

SARAH: Well, maybe it was an accident, Mom. I'll understand. Just tell me the truth and we'll tell the authorities, and we'll deal with it.

FLORENCE: (*Pauses, then gets up and slowly walks a few steps toward the Banyan tree with one crutch. Sarah immediately follows and hands her the other crutch to use.*) There're so many things I'd miss about this place, Sarah, but you know what I'd really miss? Not the house—that's just wood, cement, paint. I'd miss Buddy, the Banyan tree. Remember when you named him? I've watched that tree send all of those vines down one by one and anchor them to grow another arm for itself. Remember climbing that tree every night and staying up there so long? You used to tie notes onto a vine and lower them down and ask us to send you up food via your self-made pulley system.

SARAH: (*nostalgic*) Yeah, I used to feel safe up there.

FLORENCE: Well this is where I feel safe, Sarah. Right here on the bay.

SARAH: Mom, the neighbors are all selling!

FLORENCE: I don't need them.

SARAH: Mom, I didn't want to tell you this, but maybe you better sit down.

FLORENCE: I'm not a child, Sarah, quit babying me, and tell me what those old farts are up to. I know they're calling you.

SARAH: Mom, they say that if you don't sell I should have you committed, something about a Baker's Act—that you might be harmful to yourself.

FLORENCE: Oh my God, they've gone too far. Sarah do you really think I'd do that to you? That I'd let you come into this house and find me dead? I'm lonely sure, I miss your father ... God I miss your father. I've been stuck in this house so long it's a wonder I'm not crazy, but I'm not and you know it!

SARAH: Mom, calm down. I didn't say I believed them. It's just that they're all ready to sell to that developer. And, once they've made up their minds, they're ready to go ... so, they're talking about you. (*pause*) They say you're "touched." They say you ... talk to your refrigerator. They've seen you, Mom, through the window.

FLORENCE: (*Shakes her head. Gets up.*) No, I'm not "touched" Sarah, that's the problem. Yes, I talk to my refrigerator, and I've named her too. Remember when you used to name everything? The tree, your bike, and when you were 16 you named the car. Did that make you crazy? No, it was cute. I'll tell you something, Sarah. At night when it's quiet and the TV's off, I walk over and I don't just talk to Amana, but I hug her! As mad as your father and I got at each other at times, we found times to touch ... to hug ... humans need that. When I hug Amana and tell her to keep on running, I feel the vibration and the energy, and at least it's something.

SARAH: I'm sorry Mom, I know you're not crazy, but maybe you just need to talk to someone. I know a good doctor. He specializes in marriage counseling, but I could ask him for a name.

FLORENCE: You and Rick are having problems aren't you?

SARAH: Mom, it'll be OK. Even if we split, I'm young; I'll find someone else.

FLORENCE: I wasn't thinking of you as much as Sammi.

SARAH: She'll always be with me, Mom, no matter what happens.

FLORENCE: Sarah, she worships Rick, and she's only four. If you split now it would rock her world.

SARAH: She's strong, Mom, and Rick is gone most of the time anyway. So many kids' parents are divorced now-a-days.

FLORENCE: So, you're already thinking divorce. Sarah, marriage is hard work, and you need to think what's best for Sammi.

SARAH: I will Mom, like I said we're going to counseling—Rick agreed. (*pause*) If we did split, could we move back in awhile? I mean Rick and I would have to give up the house.

FLORENCE: I get the picture now. If I take the $500,000 and buy a nice, new condo you can move in with me, take care of Sammi and also manage all of my affairs.

SARAH: You're jumping to conclusions, Mom. (*pause*) We need to talk about the contract. $500,000, Mom! (*no response*) I have to know about "underneath." What did you mean? If Daddy didn't kill something who did?

FLORENCE: No one.

SARAH: Then what's "underneath" that would keep you here?

FLORENCE: I'm afraid to tell you, because you really will think I'm crazy.

SARAH: (*getting excited*) If there's something buried underneath this deck, I deserve to know!

FLORENCE: (*pause*) You know I've been stuck in this house for three months, nothing to do but feel sorry for myself and worry about this whole buy-out mess. But, I started fooling with your Daddy's laptop, first just emailing thank you's and then "surfing," I guess you call it. I'd bring my coffee out here in the mornings with the laptop. When the sun would come up over the big pines, I'd always look out at the shimmer on the bay and sometimes see the fin of a dolphin. Your Daddy and I used to have a contest, seeing who could count the most dolphins during the day. He cheated a lot, but I didn't care—it seems important for a man to win.

SARAH: Daddy did love to play games! And win!

FLORENCE: One morning I was standing here on this deck feeling sorry for myself, staring out at the water, and something caught my eye, something moving in the yard. Pretty soon it moved closer, eating grass. Oblivious to my presence, it came within ten feet of the deck and then disappeared.

SARAH: What was it, Mom?

FLORENCE: I have a picture of one on my laptop. Come here.

SARAH: (*Walks over, looks, and, in shock*) A turtle?

FLORENCE: A tortoise, Sarah, a gopher tortoise. Don't they look prehistoric? They're superb earthmovers. They burrow in the ground. They come out in the sun, eat grass, and they go back in their tunnels that can be up to 47 feet long. They can live up to 50 years or more. And Sarah, they've been on earth for over 60 million years, and they're here on this property, probably right under this deck as we speak. (*really trying to sell her*) If those contractors buy this house, they'll tear it down and pour concrete all over for those condos, and I know what will happen to these guys. There's more than one, Sarah, I've seen five or six walking around in the sun. They lift up their shells when they walk almost like they're on their toes. They can go quite fast when they want.

SARAH: (*extremely agitated*) You mean to tell me you're turning down $500,000 for a couple of turtles? Mom, have you lost it?

FLORENCE: I told you you'd think I was crazy. I've joined a group online that's trying to save them. Their status has just been moved from "species of special concern" to "threatened."

SARAH: Mom, sell the place and send the group $1,000, and you'll feel better. (*Florence shakes her head.*) You know I could almost understand you if Daddy really had killed someone and buried them, but reptiles? Not even mammals, Mom!

FLORENCE: Sarah, when the contractors are told there are gopher tortoises here, they have a choice between paying money or relocating them. They rarely choose relocation because they're too hard to get out of their burrows, and they'd never get them all. So they usually pay the fine. They call this an "incidental take." So, they bulldoze the land, pour concrete, and entomb them, Sarah. Starting soon they can't do that anymore. They will have to relocate them, but like I said they can't get them all. How are they going to know if they're leaving some behind? I have this reoccurring dream where I see this tortoise coming up to the surface and scratching on the concrete from underneath.

SARAH: That's not a pretty picture. But you can't save all the gopher tortoises in the world.

FLORENCE: No, but I might be able to save these few for a short while. (*pause*) You know maybe this was God's plan. Maybe that's why I stepped in a hole and fell. Maybe it was one of their holes. Maybe that's why I stopped feeling sorry for myself and focused on something I could do, a living creature I could help.

SARAH: But Mom, the neighbors!

FLORENCE: I don't care about the neighbors, Sarah! You think Harold's any more sane than I am? Talk about "touched!" Why, I've seen him shoot at Muscovy ducks right through the top of his pool cage. (*pause*) Sarah, what's happened to you? As a child you would have taken this on as an adventure. You would have stood still for hours in order to see one, and then the first thing you would have done is given it a name, "Gerald Gopher Tortoise" or "Germaine Gopher Tortoise."

SARAH: Life happened, Mom. I don't have time....I work, I take care of Sammi, I cook and clean, and, if I'm lucky, I sleep.

FLORENCE: Sounds like you don't make much time for Rick either.

SARAH: It's just so hard, Mom. (*tears in eyes*) It's so hard to be an adult.

FLORENCE: I know, Sarah. (*pause*) Shhhh ... look over there by Buddy. There's one.

SARAH: I see it! What's it doing?

FLORENCE: It's looking for just the right grass. See? Now it's eating. (*excited*) There's another one. See how they walk? Isn't it a scream?

SARAH: Yeah, I guess they're kind of cute.

FLORENCE: I knew you'd think so, Sarah. Sometimes what's underneath is more important than everything else.

SARAH: I love you, Mom.

FLORENCE: I love you too, Babe. (*They hug.*) I've missed that. The genuine touch, the hug, of another human being. (*Sarah walks over and tears up the contract.*) Thanks. (*Sarah starts to leave.*) Sarah? (*She stops and turns back around to her.*) Do you think you could bring Sammi over Saturday morning? I haven't spent quality time with her in so long. While I'm with her, why don't you put your kayak in and go out in the bay? You love kayaking, Sarah, and you haven't been since Daddy died. You never know what you might see out there, and it'll clear your mind.

SARAH: Maybe that's what I need to do ... hit delete and start over.

FLORENCE: Maybe Sammi and I will see one of the gopher tortoises.

SARAH: I'll tell her to have some names ready.

(*Sarah exits. Florence smiles and looks off towards the bay.*)

(*Blackout*)

END OF PLAY

Ten-Minute Play Festival

March 27, 28 & 29
April 3, 4 & 5, 2009

The 2009 Festival, entitled "Sailing Turbulent Seas," was performed in the historic Crocker Memorial Church. For the first time, the Festival ran over two weekends with the final performance adjudicated by Jack Eddleman, Marty Fugate and Jim Hoskins. The announcement of the award was made after that afternoon performance.

STORMY by Walton Beacham won for Best Play. The cash award was was sponsored by the Longboat Key Club & Resort.

Directors included Preston Boyd, Dan Greene, Rosalind Cramer and Laurie Zimmerman. Actors included Seva Anthony, Monia Joblin, Dylan Jones, Melliss Kenworthy, Patrick McCall, Sandra Musicante, William Muzzillo, Mike Pisacreta and Fred Zimmerman.

2009 Best Play

Stormy

by

Walton Beacham

Directed by Dan Greene

with

Fred Zimmerman as Phil
Dylan Jones as Theo
William Muzzillo as Hank

CHARACTERS

PHIL, a man in his forties, job supervisor
THEO: a man in his twenties, an art student
HANK, a man in his forties, job supervisor
Male CHORUS, off-stage

SETTING

A construction site.

TIME

The present.

* * *

Lights up.

Theo and Phil are talking with Phil gesturing toward the fourth wall, which represents an unseen billboard.

PHIL: How big is that billboard?

THEO: Big enough for the men to notice.

PHIL: I'll say! Is she that sexy in real life?

THEO: Sexier. I toned her down for the crew. Contractor said I should reward the guys, not stop 'em dead in their tracks. Said we need to improve morale around here. (*pause*) I gave her beautiful eyes so they'd look more at her face. Have you noticed how she stares at you from every angle?

PHIL: Like the Bud girls. It's spooky how you can't escape their eyes. It's like they're watching you all the time, suspicious you'll do something wrong. What's this girl's name?

THEO: Maria, but you guys should name her whatever you want. I call her Mona Lisa because of her smile.

PHIL: We'll call her Stormy—you know, for the porn star.

THEO: Couldn't be a more appropriate name than Stormy.

PHIL: Why? Is Stormy a weather girl?

THEO: She'll let you know when it rains.

PHIL: Let me know what?

THEO: Ever been to a wet-T-shirt contest.

PHIL: Sure. There's one at the Beaver Club every Wednesday night. Is Maria a contestant?

THEO: I don't think so.

PHIL: So what's she doing being cheesecake for construction workers?

THEO: Nude modeling is an honorable tradition in art.

PHIL: She modeled for you nude?

THEO: Trust me buddy. Morale is about to improve.

(*Lights dim, then rise. Hank and Phil are gesturing toward the billboard.*)

PHIL: An art student erected it Saturday. Said Sam commissioned it.

HANK: Erect's what she'll do all right.

PHIL: The artist says he reduced her breasts.

HANK: Look at the muscles in her thighs. How would you like to have those boa constrictor legs wrapped around you?

PHIL: Stormy stares at me everywhere I go. It's like she knows my every move and I can't put anything over on her.

HANK: Like what? What's the worse thing you've ever done?

PHIL: Cheated on Sarah when she was pregnant. She couldn't care less about sex. Nothing suited her.

HANK: You didn't leave her or anything?

PHIL: Didn't even consider it but I felt guilty anyway. She was home throwing up while I was out diddling. Stormy makes me nervous.

HANK: Sarah's still throwing up?

PHIL: Not because she's pregnant. Can you believe Mary's seventeen now? (*pointing at the billboard*) Got a body like Stormy's.

HANK: I don't get how artists can keep on painting when the model's lying there naked.

PHIL: Maybe artists look at women differently.

HANK: You're saying art's more important to them than sex?

PHIL: All I'm saying is it's playing with fire to put a fox on a job site even if she's just paint.

HANK: It's an art school, Phil. I'll bet there's naked women up in those studios (*points upward*) this very minute.

PHIL: So you regard Stormy as art, different from sex?

HANK: Sex is art.

PHIL: Have you ever seen this model? She could be a student here.

HANK: Stormy's pretty, real pretty, and if I saw a girl who looked like her I'd pay attention. I especially like her sassy black hair and green eyes. Sort of pulls your focus north of the hills and valley. You can see she's telling the painter something important. She's wise beyond her age.

PHIL: Is she wise or is he, the painter?

HANK: If I ever see her, I'll ask.

(*Lights dim, then rise. Hank and Phil are looking up toward the sky and gesturing about the rain.*)

HANK: Supposed to rain all day.

PHIL: How many men didn't show up this morning?

HANK: Everybody's here, plus four new guys looking for work. They heard about Stormy.

PHIL: She looks different today.

HANK: Must be the rain. Sunlight made her skin dazzle.

PHIL: It's almost like she's crying.

HANK: It's just rain running down her face. We've got a serious front moving in. Might as well send the guys home.

PHIL: (*picks up a bullhorn*) Go home men. Too much rain. (*to HANK*) Nobody's leaving.

HANK: Turn up the volume.

PHIL: (*louder*) Go home men. No pay today.

HANK: My god, Phil! Look at Stormy's bikini. It's washing away. The paint's running off the billboard. No wonder they're not leaving.

PHIL: (*again using the bullhorn*) Go home men.

HANK: That art student must have bought his paint from that same sorry dealer who sold us the bad lot. Look how it's washing off like it was water colors. You can see one of her nipples poking out.

PHIL: Doesn't make sense that only her halter's washing off. Every can of paint he sold us was old. Her whole body should be running together.

HANK: Could be just the yellow paint that's defective.

PHIL: How long is it supposed to rain?

HANK: All day. It's gonna get worse.

PHIL: If the yellow paint keeps running ... My god Hank. Look. He didn't just paint a bikini on his model, he painted her body first and then a bikini over it. You know what's gonna happen don't you? We're going to have a buck naked woman on our hands.

HANK: She's a pretty girl all right.

PHIL: The rain's coming down harder.

HANK: Look at those knockers.

PHIL: I get it Hank. The yellow paint's not defective. The kid used water soluble paints for her halter. That's why he said it would be like a wet T -shirt contest. The wetter she gets the more you see.

CHORUS: (*offstage*) Stormy!

PHIL: (*speaks in the bullhorn*) Cool it guys.

CHORUS: (*offstage cheers and moans*) Goooo Stormy!

HANK: Looks like her bottom's starting to run, too.

CHORUS: (*offstage, much louder cheers*) Hubba, hubba, hubba!

HANK: Look Phil, a crowd's gathering across the street, and television vans are pulling in. We'll all be fired.

PHIL: (*frantically to HANK*) Take her down. Tell the men to take her down. (*using the bullhorn*) Report to the service platform men. We're taking her down.

CHORUS: (*offstage loud protests*) Go Stormy. Go Stormy.

HANK: Look, Phil, her bottom's disappearing. You can see her . . . you can see everything.

CHORUS: (*offstage*) Stormee. Stormee.

HANK: Every crevice.

PHIL: We've got to get rid of her fast. (*pause*) Call the fire department, Hank. They can wash her down faster than the rain. They can make her disappear.

HANK: I'm not calling the fire department. I've got to face the men every morning.

PHIL: Now her hair's washing away, and her eyes. She's turning into a blue-eyed blonde.

HANK: That's my type. Watermelon boobs, honey maple hair, sky blue eyes. What a knockout. Let's bring her inside so she doesn't run any more.

PHIL: She looks like somebody.

HANK: Of course she looks like somebody. She is somebody. She's Stormy, our goddess.

PHIL: (*horrified*) Oh my god Hank! Look! That's Mary. That's her tattoo. That son-of-a-bitch has painted a forty foot portrait of my daughter naked. I'm calling the fire department.

HANK: Mary has a tattoo?

PHIL: A yellow flower on her left breast. She was in rebellion when she did it. Hated her mother. (*pulls cell phone from his pocket*)

HANK: No Phil. Don't call the fire department. Don't wash her away. We'll cover her up with a tarp and tell the men they can look at her at the end of every day the job goes good.

PHIL: (*dials his cell phone*) Hello, Captain. We've got an emergency at the art college. We need you to hose down a woman on a billboard. (*pause*) What do you mean the fire chief has to sign off? You don't understand, we have a gigantic pornographic woman over here at the school (*pause*) You want dean to sign off too? (*to HANK*) Get the fire hose. We'll wash her off ourselves. (*to Stormy*) He said your name is Maria but he was lying to me. It's you Mary. You've been screwing that art student and now he's exposed you.

HANK: I don't like this. We can't destroy his creation. She's our girl.

PHIL: (*desperately*) Get the fire hose. (*HANK exits. PHIL addresses the portrait*) How could you have done it Mary? I know you're furious with your mother but this is way over the edge. She doesn't like you being in art college and she'll stop paying your tuition. What will you do then? Become a pole dancer?

HANK: (*returning with fire hose*) Maybe he's immortalizing her. There's not a man here today who'll ever forget this moment. It's a life-changing experience. Mary has a beautiful blonde bush.

PHIL: Shut up, Hank. Hose it.

HANK: If I do, the men won't come to work tomorrow.

PHIL: Screw the men. Get closer, Hank. See if you can increase the pressure.

HANK: I don't think that'll help. Her legs are washing away but her nipples and her. . . Look, Phil, her stomach's disappearing, and her neck, but her face is brilliant as ever.

CHORUS: (*offstage*) Stormee. Stormee.

PHIL: Some of the men have seen Mary on campus. They must know it's her.

HANK: Well if they do she's in three parts now: disembodied. Down to her bare essentials.

PHIL: What could she have done for him to take this revenge?

HANK: It's what artists do. They show the essence of people.

PHIL: He's robbed her of her innocence. She's only seventeen. Practically statutory rape.

HANK: Face it, Phil, Mary's been screwing around and Dad's in the dark. Seventeen's not so young. Had to happen sometime.

PHIL: It's like he's sent her to the stocks in a public display of humiliation.

HANK: If we hose her long enough, what will be the last body part showing?

PHIL: What do you mean?

HANK: Some part has to be last. My guess is it's not her elbow.

PHIL: He wouldn't do that to her, would he? She's such a sweet girl.

HANK: What's more insulting than calling a woman a bitch? A c...

PHIL: Don't you dare call her that.

HANK: Ok, but that'll be the last thing we see.

(*PHIL dials a number on his cell.*)

PHIL: Mary, some asshole art student has painted you naked. You're forty feet long, or you were until everything washed away but your face and your ... your ... (*pause*) You know he painted you? (*pause*)
You're watching it on television? You think he's making a statement about mutability. What the hell is that? Why did you pose for him? (*pause*) Playboy's doing a feature on artists' models and Theo's sending them photos. (*hangs up angrily, grabs the fire hose and turns it on the portrait*) Take that you little c... (*stops himself*)

CHORUS: (*offstage, moans*) There go her eyes. (*more moans*) There go her nipples. (*more moans*) There goes her ... noooo.

(*Lights dim, then rise*)

HANK: Fooled us, didn't he. Only thing left is her smile. She's telling us how happy she is to be his model. To be his lover. To be herself. What will you do if she turns up in Playboy?

PHIL: She wouldn't dare.

HANK: She's naked on a forty-foot billboard.

PHIL: Only thing to do is turn the page. It's the only solution in life.

HANK: Trouble with Playboy is that when you turn the page and hold her to the light you still see her image through the paper. Her details are fuzzy but it's like the girl will not let go of you. Once you've tasted her sensuality you're hers. You can wash away the body but never the memory of her smiling at you, and only you, even though you know a million other men have lusted for her too.

PHIL: They can lust for her all they want but you know what Hank, they'll never know Mary, they'll never turn the page, never look at her from the inside out.

(*Blackout*)

END OF PLAY

And Gods Cry, Too

by

Janis R. Frawley

Directed by Laurie Zimmerman

with

Seva Anthony as Selwa
Dylan Jones as Joey

CHARACTERS

JOEY, a nineteen-year-old male U.S. soldier. He is exhausted, mentally defeated, filled with sorrow and guilt, and holds an inner anger bordering on hostility.

SELWA, an Iraqi woman in her forties. Grieving, yet bold and infuriated, she possesses an inner anger and hatred.

SETTING

A bench surrounded by the debris of a home that once stood on this spot in a bombed-out area of Fallujah, Iraq.

TIME

The end of December 2004.

* * *

Lights up.

Covered in the grime of battle, JOEY sits alone with his rifle. He is hunched over a dirty helmet lying in his lap, with his head in his hands that also hold a crumpled letter. Sniper fire and occasional grenades are heard in a far-off background; the prayer call of a mosque rings out.

JOEY: (*Sits up, re-reads part of the letter to himself, then crumples the paper in his hand.*) God damned this frigging war! I should be home, putting my arms around my mom ... giving her hope that we'll get through this together. (*pause*) Ah, shit! What fucking, rotten timing! (*starts to cry*)

(*In response to the sobbing she hears, SELWA, dressed in dirty, tattered cultural dress, cautiously appears from behind the scraps of what was once a dresser. She is scavenging what she can use from the debris, which includes a tattered baby doll, shoes, etc.*)

SELWA: What is that noise? You!!!! (*Hurls a shoe at him.*)

JOEY: (*ducking*) What the ...!

SELWA: Get out of here. If anyone sees me this close to the likes of you, it is death for me. Go! Go now!

JOEY: (*trying to compose himself*) I ... I'm sorry, ma'am. It's just that I ... I need a little time for myself. A little solitude. I just need to sit ... and rest ... and think.

SELWA: Leave this minute! If something happens to me, I cannot bear to think of what would become of my little girl. I am the only one left to care for her ... to protect her in this war ravaged city. No one, not even the little ones, are safe since you Americans arrived. Law is gone; order is a thing of the past. Get out of my sight! (*Throws the other shoe at him.*)

JOEY: (*blocking himself from the shoe*) Give me a break! All I want is five freakin' minutes alone. I need a sense of peace and quiet. (*anger mounting*) I had that until you showed up, giving me a ration of shit!

SELWA: (*with hatred*) We all need a sense of peace, young soldier. We women would love to stroll our streets with no fear of being assaulted or worse! We long for the days when our children can once again walk to school without being afraid! Ha! What am I saying? Our schools now lay in piles of rubble ... just like the souls of our children ... The young who are left alive look at life through dimmed, hopeless eyes; the others lay buried without even getting a chance at life ... All because your kind came invading our country and pushing yourselves on us!

JOEY: (*anger mounting*) My kind, huh? Yea, like it's a picnic for my kind to be here – never knowing which one of your kind is going to blow up our bodies beyond recognition. And don't tell me about hopeless, lifeless eyes. I've looked into too many of my buddies' eyes who have had their limbs blown off by those who don't appreciate the sacrifices we're making for you people.

SELWA: We are supposed to appreciate you destroying our lives? We never asked for your sacrifices or your help. You were never invited here. Our oil was the prize your ...

JOEY: Don't even go there. Are you forgetting that Iraqi's cheered and danced in the streets when we brought down Saddam?

SELWA: Those that cheered could never begin to imagine the destruction and wrenching heartache you would leave in your wake. We hoped you would be gone by now to let us plot our own course.

JOEY: (*anger swelling*) Listen, lady, I don't want to be here anymore than you want me here. I'm damned sick to death of it all! I want to be home ... with my mom ... eating apple pie ... hanging out in my own room, riding my bike around the neighborhood. It's always been just me and my mom ... making life feel good for each other. She begged me not to enlist, but we're poor and always struggling. I thought if I enlisted ...

SELWA: You do not know the meaning of struggle! Two of my young sons and my parents died when your bombs blew up our home. My husband is off somewhere ... fighting, or maybe dead. Your soldiers arrested my oldest son and sent him to prison in Abu Ghraib just for stealing a little food for us to eat. (*softer, sadly*) A prison guard fired a machine gun into his genitals and left him to die a slow death over a period of days. May Allah strike all of you dead! You are all dogs! Now it is just me and my precious little Jamila and we have only Allah to rely upon. (*pause*) Let me ask you, what is the nature of this Christian God who told your President Bush to do this to the people of my country?

JOEY: To be honest, ... my Jesus, my God, wouldn't have told him to do any of this. What I've seen, and done, turns my stomach. It all goes against everything my church, and my mom, ever taught me.

SELWA: Aaah! So he falsely puts the blame for his own actions onto your Christian God! The women at the well say Bin Ladin, too, boasts that what he does is for our Allah. They think your Bush and Bin Ladin are alike ... two evil men who think nothing of killing, maiming, and tearing lives apart, yet both claim to be so holy. That, young soldier, goes against everything my mother ever taught me.

JOEY: Didn't Saddam's cruelty go against everything your mom ever taught you? President Bush liberated you from all that.

SELWA: Cruel? Yes, he was. But at least our lives were whole back then. We had homes and families and dreams. Our children played in the streets, ate ice cream and slept safely in their own beds. They prepared to make something of their lives in school. We could laugh and love. We had good food, petrol for our cars, and medical care. All we have now are hollow hearts and broken lives impossible to repair. The price of this so-called freedom has been too high.

JOEY: (*very angry*) My God, woman! We have American families whose lives were blown apart on 9-11, too. They no longer laugh or love. Muslims did that. You Muslims are the reason I'm in this God-forsaken hell-hole while my mom is home battling cancer all by herself.

SELWA: (*somberly*) Think clearly, boy. Not one of those Muslims involved in your 9-11 was Iraqi.

JOEY: (*defensively*) No, but a lot of Muslims hate America, so we vowed to rid the world of Saddam's weapons of ...

SELWA: (*a sad laugh*) My country had no weapons of mass destruction. The whole world knew that ... including your ruler.

JOEY: My ruler, as you call him, took an honorable step toward wiping out terrorism ...

SELWA: He came to the wrong place for that, too! Saddam never allowed terrorists to raise their ugly heads in his country. Our land now crawls thick with them.

JOEY: Our duty as American soldiers is to go where our commander-in-chief sends us. We're giving up our youth and our lives to bring democracy to your part of the world. It's an admirable thing.

SELWA: You had better just keep an opened eye on your own democracy ... and leave others to govern themselves.

JOEY: My purpose for being here is to make life better for you and your little girl ...

SELWA: Better? Listen to me, my young, naive soldier. Do any Americans ever think of asking how many innocent children, mothers, and grandparents have died because your president supposedly wanted to make our lives better? Have you ever wondered ... or even asked? Do you know how many innocents have died in this war?

JOEY: (*defensively, but with a bit of shame*) I don't have to count the bodies. I see it every day.

SELWA: (*anger mounting*) Aaah! I did not think you would know. Your government keeps that a secret, do they not? The body count of innocent deaths far exceeds 100,000, and that is without counting those who died right here in the massacre of my Fallujah. (*pause*) The world rose and collectively mourned the 100,000 who died in the Asian tsunami. They cried for them ... they supplied food, water, and medicine to those who somehow survived. Order was quickly restored there. Here, whether dead or alive, we are forgotten by the world. (*Pauses, takes a deep breath, and a strong sense of sorrow sets in.*) I heard that people in many countries lit candles in respect for the poor victims of the tsunami. Does anyone, anywhere, ever even think of lighting a candle, or pausing for a moment of silence for our dead babies? Or to even say a prayer for them? (*pause*) Do they ever give thought to the grief devouring the souls of Iraqi survivors? Do they ask about the Iraqi mothers who have lost their beloved children ... their husbands ... or their parents? (*Waits for him to respond, but he doesn't.*) We, the Iraqi mothers, are the forgotten people in George Bush's war. We are the ones no one reflects upon.

JOEY: (*at the end of his rope*) OK, lady, I don't know why I'm here. I had no idea how many innocent Iraqis have died. I'm sorry! I'm so damned sorry. Oh, God, my head feels like it's gonna bust wide open. (*pause*) I had to look into a young man's eyes and kill him today. I'm not a killer. They don't even give me the things I need so I don't get killed. Do you know what that feels like? Sacrificial fodder and I'm so damned angry about it that my heart feels like it's going to implode! (*His anger turns to sadness.*) My best friend ... two days ago I drug him from a burning humvee that was only protected by scraps of metal we had to rummage through trash heaps to find. I can't get his face out of my mind. Oh, Jesus, it won't go away ... (*Tears roll down his face.*) All that I've seen ... all that I've been forced to do ... and now this letter from my mom. (*anger rising*) I can't take much more. I want to go home. I need to wake up in my own bed and feel the warmth of my dog lying beside me. I need to look out my bedroom window and see the moss dripping from the oak trees. Most of all I need my mom ... and, God knows, my mom needs me. And I can't get to her because I'm here in this ffffucking hell hole. Oh, Jesus, help me! I need my mom.

(*As JOEY slumps over and starts crying, SELWA sees blood seeping from a gunshot wound in his back. She steps toward him with her hand outstretched to touch his shoulder. But she resists this motherly urge and steps back.*)

SELWA: I need my precious sons.

(*She turns her back on him and begins to walk away. She hesitates, then turns and walks toward him, kneeling down beside him and tenderly putting her arm around this soldier who she now sees as just a young boy in need. He puts his arms around her, as if she were his own mother, and buries his head in her shoulder and sobs. She holds him lovingly as he cries. She begins to stroke his hair as tears stream down her face.*)

Go ahead and cry ... my son. I think our Gods are crying, too.

(*Blackout*)

END OF PLAY

Lost and Found

by

Jenny Beres

Directed by Rosalind Cramer

with

Monia Joblin as Karen
Dylan Jones as Young Man

CHARACTERS

KAREN, a woman in her late twenties
YOUNG MAN, a man in his twenties

SETTING

The Lost and Found of a swanky hotel restaurant.

TIME

The present.

* * *

Lights up.

KAREN sits behind the counter, on the telephone, rummaging through a box of items that have been left behind.

She is on the phone with a customer, who is apparently very upset.

KAREN: Tortoise shell. Rectangular lenses. Very expensive.

(*KAREN sifts through the box and pulls out a pair of glasses, like the ones just described. She puts them on her face.*)

KAREN: I'm sorry ma'am nothing like that has turned up.

(*Karen pulls out a hand mirror and examines her reflection in great detail.*)

KAREN: I always find it helpful to carefully retrace my steps. Have you checked on top of your head- please hold there's another call-

(*Karen clicks over.*)

KAREN: Thank you for calling the Swan Hotel and Restaurant where luxury seems to float on by. How may I direct your call? (*pause*) Yes, one second while I connect you.

(*Karen puts the receiver down for a moment, and checks her teeth in the mirror for a few seconds before again picking up the receiver.*)

KAREN: Hello, Lost and Found. Mm hmm, blue you say? 200 per cent cashmere? I do hope we find it.

(*Karen ducks out of sight behind the counter. She is heard frantically rummaging around the items. She reappears still wearing the glasses wrapped in a royal blue, thick, cashmere scarf.*)

KAREN: (*into the receiver*) Ma'am nothing has turned up yet. A Christmas gift? Well December is right around the corner again, perhaps you could request another? Anytime. Thank you for calling.

(*KAREN clicks over to the original call.*)

KAREN: Were you still holding for the Lost and Found? The glasses. That's right. I will make a note.

(*KAREN makes zero effort to make a note. She continually has to adjust the glasses which are clearly too big for her face throughout the phone call.*)

KAREN: Ladies glasses, uh huh, Versace. Oh? That was just a guess. You sound like woman with fine taste and good diction. Isn't that a Versace woman, no doubt? Room 502. Got it. I will call if they turn up. Thank you for staying at the Swan. Where we never ruffle your feathers.

(*KAREN hangs up the phone-exhausted. A YOUNG MAN approaches the desk.*)

YOUNG MAN: Is this the Lost and Found?

KAREN: Sort of.

YOUNG MAN: What?

KAREN: (*smiling*) How may I help you?

YOUNG MAN: My wife ...

KAREN: Have you tried the Ladies Lounge. 4th floor?

YOUNG MAN: She's not lost.

KAREN: (*trying to get rid of him*) Couples counseling, 8th floor.

YOUNG MAN: No ...

KAREN: No? Then she's better off without you-

YOUNG MAN: I mean no, that's not what I mean. I've lost my wedding band.

KAREN: With or without the finger?

YOUNG MAN: Please, I already feel terrible.

KAREN: So I'm guessing without.

YOUNG MAN: You're judging me.

KAREN: I just work here. For minimum wage. I don't have a balance big enough to judge the higher tax brackets.

YOUNG MAN: She's going to kill me. Look, I'm sweating.

KAREN: Gross. Fitness center, 6th floor.

YOUNG MAN: This is going to sound crazy but I just wanted to remember what circulation in my ring finger felt like.

KAREN: And how did it feel?

YOUNG MAN: Like I was lost without it.

KAREN: How uncanny.

YOUNG MAN: I never would cheat! I've never not been married. I was a baby, then a boy, then married.

KAREN: You don't have to explain yourself to me.

YOUNG MAN: I do. I can see you're a Christian.

KAREN: Oh my God. I'm starting to look like Jesus?

YOUNG MAN: I didn't say you looked like CHRIST. I said Christian.

KAREN: What does that even mean?

YOUNG MAN: You look nice - and outwardly judgmental.

KAREN: It must be the glasses. They're not mine.

YOUNG MAN: I love my wife. You have to believe me.

KAREN: You do seem panicked. But again, I'm not the one you need to be confessing to.

YOUNG MAN: You're right. Take off the glasses.

KAREN: Okay.

(*KAREN removes the glasses.*)

KAREN: Is that better?

YOUNG MAN: (*groaning*) A little.

KAREN: Well, what does the ring look like?

YOUNG MAN: Very simple. Pretty. Platinum. A stack of diamonds.

KAREN: And your wife?

YOUNG MAN: Pretty. Platinum. Also stacked.

KAREN: Any special inscriptions?

YOUNG MAN: (*fondly*) She has my name tattooed on her ass.

KAREN: Wow. I actually meant on the ring.

YOUNG MAN: (*embarrassed*) To my darling Max, love Estelle.

KAREN: Well Max, I haven't ...

YOUNG MAN: I'm not Max.

KAREN: Who the hell are you then?

YOUNG MAN: Howard.

KAREN: OK Howard, why then do you have Max's ring?

YOUNG MAN: I'm married to his first wife.

KAREN: And she came with his ring?

YOUNG MAN: And that's about all. Son of a bitch took everything else even the dog.

KAREN: Men and their dogs.

YOUNG MAN: A poodle too, of all things. Broke Estelle's heart when she found out Max lost her. Poor Frankie.

KAREN: How does somebody lose a dog?

YOUNG MAN: (*shamefully*) I don't know. How does someone lose their wedding ring?

KAREN: Or anything- I tell you, business has been booming.

YOUNG MAN: You get any tips?

KAREN: Oh you know, here and there.

YOUNG MAN: So now what?

KAREN: (*exasperated*) I don't know. I'm the Lost and Found. What's next? You going to ask the coat check to service your car?

YOUNG MAN: (*whining*) You have to help me.

KAREN: Why?

YOUNG MAN: Because if I come home without a ring, she's going to kill me.

KAREN: How bad could it be? Just explain to her-

YOUNG MAN: (*worried laugh*) You can't explain anything to this woman.

KAREN: I'm sure you're exaggerating.

YOUNG MAN: She doesn't stop screaming long enough to explain. The Mrs. has three volumes: loud, louder and loudest.

KAREN: (*giving in*) Fine. Let me see what I have back here.

(*Karen ducks behind the counter and is heard rummaging around.*)

YOUNG MAN: What are you doing?

KAREN: Trying to save your marriage. Though, traditionally that is done in one of our deluxe suites.

YOUNG MAN: Thanks. If we book a room, I'll make sure you get the commission.

(*KAREN reappears from behind the counter. She is holding a ring in her hand.)*

YOUNG MAN: That's not it.

KAREN: I know that. But it's the best I can do. Do you want it or not?

YOUNG MAN: It doesn't look anything like my ring!

KAREN: It even has an inscription. A universal one. "To my darling wife, love Pookie."

YOUNG MAN: It's a woman's ring?

KAREN: You have very dainty fingers.

YOUNG MAN: Lord.

KAREN: I'm working with limited resources here. I'm not a pawn shop. I only have what people leave behind. Do you want the damn ring or not, Pookie?

YOUNG MAN: Fine. I'll take it.

(*KAREN also removes her glasses. She wipes the lenses and hands them to the young man.*)

KAREN: Here.

YOUNG MAN: What are these for?

KAREN: They're nice. Versace. Wrap them up and give them to her. I think they'll ease the blow.

YOUNG MAN: Are you sure?

KAREN: Absolutely. Evidently, I need a new look.

YOUNG MAN: Thank you.

(*The YOUNG MAN goes to hug KAREN, but she leans far away from the counter.*)

KAREN: (*pointing to the counter*) After ten years of therapy, I finally have boundaries.

(*The YOUNG MAN turns to leave and tips his imaginary hat. KAREN nods. The man exits.*

KAREN waits until he is totally out of sight and then she picks up the phone and dials.)

KAREN: Hello, is this room 502? Yes ma'am, I located your glasses, I just saw them walking out of the first floor going east. A young man. If you leave now you can still catch them.

(*KAREN hangs up smugly.*

Once more KAREN reaches into the box, this time pulling out the diamond ring. She slips it on her finger and admires its beauty.

The phone rings.)

KAREN: (*picking up the phone while holding her hand up to catch light*) Thank you for calling the Swan Hotel and Restaurant - where luxury is always found just beyond your reach.

(*Blackout*)

END OF PLAY

Transition

by

Larry Hamm

Directed by Laurie Zimmerman

with

Fred Zimmerman as Brian
Sandra Musicante as Erica

CHARACTERS
BRIAN, a man in his late 30's or early 40's
ERICA, a woman (any age)

SETTING
The hereafter.

TIME
The present.

*   *   *

Lights up.

ERICA sits at a desk stage left, making notes on a stack of note cards. A second smaller stack of cards sits on the desk toward the front, upstage corner. A stool is slightly right of center. A buzzer sounds and after a pause BRIAN enters through the curtain, center, clearly disoriented and shaking his head.

ERICA: Hello.

BRIAN: Uh ... this isn't where I was.

ERICA: You got that right. Do you remember where you were?

BRIAN: (thinking) Um ... I was beating the red light at the corner of Tangelo and 5th.

ERICA: Well, it beat back.

BRIAN: And I ...

ERICA: ... became something resembling ground round.

BRIAN: You mean ... those lights ...

ERICA: ... belonged to a Ford Cherokee that was jumping the green light.

BRIAN: The bastard.

ERICA: Oh, don't worry, he's dead, too. His name was Jeremy. Nice guy. Just left. Must have died instantly. Apparently, you hung on a little longer. The paramedics probably were annoyed they had to keep working on what was obviously a lost cause.

BRIAN: (*horrified*) That's pretty cold.

ERICA: Not as cold as what Jeremy had to say about you. He was rather disappointed and angry. He had been in a hurry to get home to his youngest son's birthday party. (*sighs in sadness, then back to business*) So, what's your story?

BRIAN: (*looks around, sensing where he might be for the first time*) Uh ... my story? Is that what this is about? Some sort of tribunal to determine ... uh ...

ERICA: Where your soul goes after you die?

BRIAN: Oh my God.

ERICA: (*reacts to the last word*) Not even close. Not God, nor anyone in any theological food chain. In fact, I'm no more a tribunal than I am a judge on Dancing with the Stars. I don't have a title, really. Shame. It keeps me from ordering business cards. No, this isn't some inquisition to determine punishment versus paradise. I mean, you're already dead, right? Your life was what it was. Judgment isn't necessary. What we're doing here is more like a debriefing, what the military might call an After Action Review. (*picks up the top note card from the desk*)

BRIAN: We're reviewing my life?

ERICA: It's all part of the transition. You know how people with near death experiences say that they saw their lives pass in front of their eyes? Well, this is something like that ... without the visuals.

BRIAN: (*worried*) Transition? To where?

ERICA: Don't get excited. It's not really a place, but you'll get there. Don't always be in such a hurry. Do I have to remind you about the red light?

BRIAN: Okay, but you do understand that my destination might be significant.

ERICA: Really?

BRIAN: Yes, really. We're talking about how and where I'm going to spend eternity.

ERICA: (*looks at note card*) You don't seem to have been concerned about that before.

BRIAN: (*defiantly*) That's not true. I always played by the rules. I went to church almost every Sunday. I provided for my family. I nodded to the neighbors when I saw them. I gave money to charities – cancer research ... (*beginning to grasp*) some organization rescuing animals ... something that had to do with young girls becoming women...

ERICA: (*reads in monotone from note card*) You once gave a homeless man a dollar because he made you feel uncomfortable.

BRIAN: I did? (*curious)* Is my whole life on there?

ERICA: Everything that matters.

BRIAN: It's not very big.

ERICA: (*with mock sympathy*) Size isn't important.

BRIAN: Are you mocking my life? Is that what this is about? Is that what you're supposed to be doing?

ERICA: Job descriptions here are vague. But, you're right, we really need to get down to business. After all, our relationship is clearly going nowhere. (*whispers loudly to self*) Jeremy was a LOT nicer.

BRIAN: I heard that. That's not fair. You don't even know me. (*Erica smiles and waves the card at him.*) That isn't me. I am not the sum of a bunch of things written on some card.

ERICA: (*sitting on top of desk*) So, tell me who you are. Start with anything (*offhandedly and a bit seductively*). What was your wildest fantasy?

BRIAN: Well (*Erica begins to write on the card*) ... oh, wait ... I see ... you're baiting me ... the truth is I had no wild fantasies, I was married ... I never did anything inappropriate ... I lived like I was taught to live ... I went to work every day... I believed in the American Dream ... (*proudly*) I was a Conservative. (*Erica giggles and writes*) Is there something wrong with that?

ERICA: I told you. This isn't about right or wrong. Only I always find it amusing that every self-titled Conservative I see here is praying that God is a Liberal.

BRIAN: (*a bit worried*) Isn't he?

ERICA: This isn't about a Him ... um ... (*looks at card*) Brian. Don't you get it, yet? This is about you ... who you are.

BRIAN: Well, I'm a lot better guy than you seem to think I am. People liked me.

ERICA: (*looking hard at both sides of card to find this information*) Go on.

BRIAN: They did like me. I always smiled and said good things to everyone.

ERICA: Like "have a nice day."

BRIAN: You make it sound shallow, but I did want them to have a nice day. I cared about others.

ERICA: (*looking at the card*) You cared about Justino Gutierrez, Maggie Haylock, and Nancy Williams?

BRIAN: Cared about? I didn't even know them.

ERICA: You didn't know the man who mowed your yard for the past eight years, your company's longtime receptionist, and a woman you had hot tub sex with at a Marriott outside Chicago during the 1992 Application Panel Distributor's Convention?

BRIAN: (*surprised and defensive*) Well, of course I ... they ... that was a long time ... her name was Nancy?

ERICA: Listen, Brian, I'm really not here to bust your chops, but this is it for you, your one final look at what your life may or may not have meant ... your chance to determine who you are. I think you might want to try being a little introspective and truthful. Everything I'm seeing here (*shakes card*) tells me you were pretty much a self-centered asshole, so I'm giving you about another five minutes before I move you along.

BRIAN: (*becoming emotional*) I'm going to Hell aren't I?

ERICA: Calm down. You're focusing on the wrong thing.

BRIAN: (*nearing tears*) I don't want to burn for all eternity.

ERICA: (*putting her hand on his shoulder*) It's okay, Brian. There is no burning, no fire and brimstone. No real place called Hell.

BRIAN: But the stories said ...

ERICA: I know. The stories say a lot of different things. You're supposed to read them and think about them and feel them. They're allegories meant for interpretation. Immortality is a rather big issue. You don't expect to learn about it in a five-paragraph essay, do you?

BRIAN: I guess not, but I did believe. Doesn't that count?

ERICA: Everyone believes something. Even the denial of belief is a belief of its own. What did your belief mean?

BRIAN: I did try to be a good person.

ERICA: (*correcting him*) You tried to set up rules t prove you were a good person. You were responsible and hard-working, and you thought that was all you needed to be.

BRIAN: I did. I thought that.

ERICA: And you handed over your spirit to a set of religious guidelines, manipulated to allow you to make as much money as you could and to live your life free of consequences as long as you paid some kind of homage to the claptrap of the day and slapped an ichtus symbol on the rear of your car.

BRIAN: An ichtus?

ERICA: The fish sticker.

BRIAN: I did that for Jesus.

ERICA: No, you did that for Jesus points. You know, fill up the old stamp book with superficial acts so that you can redeem it upon death.

BRIAN: (*getting a little desperate*) I just wanted to show my faith.

ERICA: By slapping a two dollar decal on a $60,000 SUV?

BRIAN: (*covers his face with his hands*) Oh, this is not going well.

ERICA: (*watches him for a moment, moves around him thinking of a new tactic*) Brian? (*he slowly uncovers his face*) Brian I've told you there are no torture chambers awaiting you. What are you so afraid of?

BRIAN: (*thinks briefly ... speaks uncertainly*) The emptiness?

ERICA: (*understanding*) What emptiness Brian?

BRIAN: (*continues to struggle for an answer*) Of a world without me.

ERICA: (*puts her hand on his shoulder*) The world will be fine.

BRIAN: (*shakes his head, sadly*) I know.

ERICA: And that bothers you?

BRIAN: (*recognizing the truth in this*) Yes. It does. It's terrible to think that the world hardly knew I existed.

ERICA: And if the entire world were in mourning, would it matter more now?

BRIAN: I suppose not. I guess I feel I didn't make much of an impact.

ERICA: Like making millions of dollars or being President?

BRIAN: No ... I don't think so ... not really ... more like devoting my life to caring for others or creating a life-saving drug.

ERICA: Not everyone is Mother Teresa or Jonas Salk.

BRIAN: But I didn't even come close. You were right about those three people who were nameless to me. There were probably hundreds more. I was paying attention to all the wrong things. I should have watched more sunsets, spent more time with friends, helped more strangers ...

ERICA: Regrets. Everyone has them.

BRIAN: But here I am at this stage of my life (*recognizes his mistake*), my afterlife, and I realize that I didn't turn out to be the person I thought I would be ... that I could have been. I don't know that person I became. I can't explain him.

ERICA: You can't care about him anymore.

BRIAN: But, who was I? Who am I?

ERICA: (*reacting to the last question*) That's what I've been asking.

BRIAN: Who I am? (*examines himself*) Maybe no one. I forget now why I was angry, why I was afraid, why I was jealous, why I ever had road rage ... rage at living. Without that I seem to be nothing, a shallow hole where I used to be, some deleted entries in co-workers' online schedules, a fading thought in the hearts of a half-dozen people.

ERICA: What you left behind isn't all nothingness.

BRIAN: (*understanding her point*) I know Julie and Shannon miss me.

ERICA: Your wife and daughter miss you? They're devastated Brian.

BRIAN: Wife? Daughter? Yes, they were. Why don't I remember them that way?

ERICA: How do you remember them?

BRIAN: (*smiles*) In fragments ... Julie's laugh and the way she'd glare sarcastically at me whenever I said anything stupid. Yet, she loved it when I'd be silly. Her cooking ... her awful cooking. She once overcooked a meatloaf until it was black. We used to say that she invented Cajun. How she enjoyed that. Cooking and laughing.

ERICA: Anything else?

BRIAN: Tons. Shannon's smile ... she's in the backseat of the car ... watching me in the rearview mirror as I drive. Maybe it was on that trip to Disney World. Maybe it was just a trip to the grocery store. Her eyes were always filled with energy, as if they had exploding constellations in them. Even when she was sad, like when our dog Charlie died, those eyes would look at me with such fire. Though she was crying I could see the source of life within them. It was my source of life. And her giggle (*trails off*) ...

ERICA: Brian?

BRIAN: I see it all. I feel it all. Walking with my Mom and Dad. I am six. (*He holds his hands upward to grab theirs.*) And Jerry?

ERICA: Your older brother.

BRIAN: The day he gave me his bike. A day at the lake. A child playing with children. And then I'm an adult looking out the window wondering at the rain. Holding Julie. Holding Shannon the day she was born. If only ...

ERICA: If only ... ?

BRIAN: If only I could hold all of them forever.

ERICA: (*Puts the note card on the desk on top the stack at the far corner.*) You will. (*Points him stage left.*) You do.

BRIAN: (*beginning to exit left*) Is it time for me to become a soul now?

ERICA: (*smiles*) Brian, you are your soul, and always have been.

(*Brian looks at Erica one last time and exits left. She watches him exit and returns to sit behind the desk, picking up a card and beginning to make notes on it. The buzzer sounds.*)

(*Blackout*)

END OF PLAY

Rights and Permissions

And Gods Cry, Too ©2009 by Janice R. Frawley. Reprinted by permission of Janice R. Frawley. For performance rights, contact Janice Frawley (theatreodyssey@gmail.com).

Claws and Effect ©2002 by Michael F. K. Phelan. Reprinted by permission of Mike Phelan. For performance rights, contact Mike Phelan (phelanmike@yahoo.com).

Delicto ©2006 by Maureen A. Martin. Reprinted by permission of Maureen A. Martin. For performance rights, contact Maureen A. Martin (mamartin@aim.com).

Dinner at the Steak Barn ©2008 by Dean Glasel. Reprinted by permission of Dean Glasel. For performance rights, contact Dean Glasel (Danddglas@aol.com).

Duct Tape ©2007 by Corinne Fleisher. Reprinted by permission of Corinne Fleisher. For performance rights, contact Corinne Fleisher (cvfleisher@aol.com).

Forgotten Memories ©2008 by Eva T. Slane. Reprinted by permission of Eva T. Slane. For performance rights, contact Eva T. Slane (gitadevi@mac.com).

Heather's Legacy ©2007 by James Hilderbrandt. Reprinted by permission of James Hilderbrandt. For performance rights, contact James Hilderbrandt (Jamesflnc@aol.com).

Lost and Found ©2009 by Jenny Beres. Reprinted by permission of Jenny Beres. For performance rights, contact Jenny Beres (jennyberes@hotmail.com).

Necessary Evil ©2000 by Michael F. K. Phelan. Reprinted by permission of Mike Phelan. For performance rights, contact Mike Phelan (phelanmike@yahoo.com).

Preconception ©2008 by Larry Hamm. Reprinted by permission of Larry Hamm. For performance rights, contact Larry Hamm (larry@larryhamm.com).

Shared Sorrow ©2008 by M. John Bohane. Reprinted by permission of M. John Bohane. For performance rights, contact M. John Bohane (mjbohane@comcast.net).

Sins of the Father ©2006 by M. John Bohane. Reprinted by permission of M. John Bohane. For performance rights, contact M. John Bohane (mjbohane@comcast.net).

Also Available from Nigel Publishing on AMAZON

Theatre Odyssey Ten-Minute Play Festival, 2010—2013 (Volume 2)

Founded in 2006 to promote the efforts of playwrights and actors on the Gulf Coast of Florida, Theatre Odyssey has premiered over 60 plays, many of which have enjoyed later productions throughout the United States. Volume 2 covers those plays from the second four years of the Festival, following the successful publication of Volume 1, 2006—2009.

Reality Show and other Short Plays

By Larry Hamm

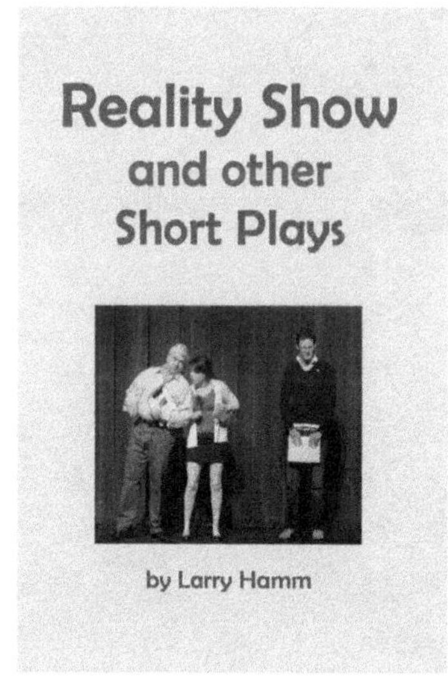

Larry Hamm's plays have won numerous awards and appeared on stages across the country and around the world. Included in this volume are PRECONCEPTION, the story of Sperm and Egg, which has been produced in Australia, New Zealand, and India as well as in countless venues in North America, and DO-OVERS, the story of a couple discussing their many reincarnations with a young soul, which has had great success as a practice piece in college classrooms.

www.ingramcontent.com/pod-product-compliance
Lightning Source LLC
LaVergne TN
LVHW010916110826
845149LV00013B/2389